UNIVERSITIES IN THE MARKETPLACE

UNIVERSITIES IN THE MARKETPLACE

THE COMMERCIALIZATION OF HIGHER EDUCATION

Derek Bok

Princeton University Press

Princeton and Oxford

Copyright © 2003 by Princeton University Press
Published by Princeton University Press, 41 William Street, Princeton,
New Jersey 08540
In the United Kingdom: Princeton University Press, 3 Market Place,
Woodstock, Oxfordshire OX20 1SY
All Rights Reserved

Fifth printing, and first paperback printing, 2005
Paperback ISBN 0-691-12012-9

THE LIBRARY OF CONGRESS HAS CATALOGED THE CLOTH EDITION
OF THIS BOOK AS FOLLOWS

Bok, Derek Curtis.
Universities in the marketplace : the commercialization of higher education /
Derek Bok.
p. cm.
Includes bibliographical references and index.
ISBN 0-691-11412-9 (alk. paper)
1. Education, Higher—Economic aspects—United States. 2. Industry
and education—United States. 3. Universities and colleges—United
States—Sociological aspects. I. Title.
LC67.62 .B65 2003
338.4'3378—dc21   2002029267

British Library Cataloging-in-Publication Data is available

This book has been composed in Electra and American Gothic

Printed on acid-free paper. ∞

pup.princeton.edu

Printed in the United States of America

5   7   9   10   8   6

CONTENTS

PREFACE

During the past twenty-five years, universities have become much more active in selling what they know and do to individuals and corporations. Commercialization of this kind is not new; it came into being many decades ago through the growth of intercollegiate athletics. As early as 1915, Yale earned more than $1 million from its football team (in current dollars). Since 1975, however, universities have been much more aggressive than they previously were in trying to make money from their research and educational activities. Many institutions have launched vigorous patent licensing programs, for-profit ventures in Internet education, and a wide variety of other commercial initiatives. In the following pages, I discuss why this trend has developed, what dangers it poses for universities, and how academic leaders can act to limit the risk to their institutions.

This is not the first time that I have discussed this topic publicly. On the fourth of June, 1988, in a commencement address before thousands of Harvard students, alumni, and friends, I raised the issue in a quite unconventional manner. Instead of describing the commercial opportunities presented to Harvard and the ways in which the institution was responding, I decided to seize the attention of the audience by broaching the subject through a wholly fictitious set of dreams that I claimed to have had only a few weeks before.

That spring, the newspapers had been full of stories about junk bonds, leveraged buy-outs, hostile takeovers, and other bizarre financial schemes. Tales of infamous figures such as Ivan Boesky and Michael Milken had dominated the financial pages. Inspired by these accounts, I in-

vented a set of dreams that started with my impulsive decision to accept the suggestion of a Harvard alumnus by bor-
rowing $2 billion to assemble the greatest faculty, the finest
facilities, and the most talented student body the world had
ever seen.

The first "dream" began at a dinner in New York where I
met the alumnus, an extravagantly successful investment
banker. After listening to my troubles raising the money to
meet Harvard's never-ending needs, he persuaded me to
take the gigantic loan. The extra $2 billion, he argued,
ought to improve the university to such a point that finding
funds to repay the loan would be easy. Weary of constantly
begging for money, I agreed.

The next and happiest "dream" saw Harvard enter a
wildly successful period. The flood of new money soon
brought world-renowned scholars, dazzling new buildings,
incredibly talented students, and other intellectual riches to
Cambridge. For once, students, faculty, and alumni lauded
my leadership, and flattering editorials appeared in the *New
York Times* and *Washington Post*. All too soon, however, my
euphoria ended. From that night on, each successive "dream"
brought forth a more difficult, more controversial scheme
to earn the money needed to meet the escalating payments
required by the loan.

I began the process modestly by vastly upgrading the athletic program: enlarging the stadium, adding luxury boxes,
and recruiting athletes good enough to put Harvard regularly on national television and into lucrative postseason
bowl games. When more money was needed to cover the
next series of payments, I turned to selling "redundant"
paintings from the Fogg Museum. Unfortunately, this
promising scheme aroused the ire of art lovers everywhere
and led to the election of several new trustees pledged to

vote for my removal if I sold a single additional picture. Undaunted, I quickly changed course and offered interested companies exclusive rights to license the discoveries in our best life-science departments, a gambit that worked well for a time, but not well enough to meet the mounting payments called for by the loan agreement. Still undismayed, I launched an ambitious for-profit distance education company to send courses via the Internet to students around the world willing to pay handsomely for a Harvard degree. Alas, although the new enterprise attracted large audiences, heavy marketing and production costs kept us from earning all the profits we needed to pay our creditors.

When I pleaded for some scheme that would at last put an end to our financial problems, my financier-alumnus came back to me with a bolder idea. What I needed to do, he said, was to allow companies (for a price) to advertise at Harvard by putting their corporate logo on syllabi and course materials, placing advertisements in classrooms, giving sales pitches to incoming students in the Business School's executive programs, and including commercials in all of our courses on television or the Internet. When I refused to accept this proposal, fearing a revolt by the senior faculty, my financial adviser was visibly irritated. Nevertheless, he returned the following night with one final proposal to spare me the public disgrace of having to default on the loan. All I had to do, he said, was to agree to set aside the last one hundred places in every entering Harvard College class and auction them off to the highest bidders.

This long, unhappy saga ended just as my financier finished explaining his final nefarious proposition. As I described it, I awoke suddenly, shaking uncontrollably, only to realize that the whole tragic cycle had been, after all, merely a dream.

What inspired me to give such a speech? Many people in the audience probably left Harvard Yard asking themselves that very question. In fact, however, I had a serious purpose that I tried to explain at the end of my address. Throughout the 1980s, deans and professors had brought me one proposition after another to exchange some piece or product of Harvard for money—often quite substantial sums of money. I will admit that I was intrigued by these opportunities, for, contrary to popular opinion, Harvard always seemed to need more resources. Nevertheless, nagging questions kept occurring to me. Was everything in the university for sale if the price was right? If more and more "products" of the university were sold at a profit, might the lure of the marketplace alter the behavior of professors and university officials in subtle ways that would change the character of Harvard for the worse?

These questions troubled me then. They trouble me still, now that the past decade has brought forth fresh reports of universities partnering with venture capitalists to sell Internet courses at a profit and medical schools taking money from pharmaceutical companies in return for allowing them to help design educational programs for physicians. Observing these trends, I worry that commercialization may be changing the nature of academic institutions in ways we will come to regret. By trying so hard to acquire more money for their work, universities may compromise values that are essential to the continued confidence and loyalty of faculty, students, alumni, and even the general public.

In writing this book, I have benefited from the comments of several people who kindly read all or part of the manuscript: David Blumenthal, Bill Bowen, Maureen Devlin, David Nathan, Henry Rosovsky, Mary Sansalone,

Michael Shinagel, James Shulman, Daniel Steiner, Lloyd
Weinreb, and Nikki Zapol. A student at the Kennedy
School, Cory Way, gave me invaluable research assistance.
Once again, my assistant, Connie Higgins, has performed
exemplary service by working through innumerable drafts; I
cannot thank her enough for her patience.

I also owe a great debt to the Rockefeller Foundation for
allowing me to write the first draft of this book in the sub-
lime surroundings of the Villa Serbelloni in Bellagio, Italy.
Under the incomparable direction of Gianna Celli, no better environment has ever been devised for thinking and
writing.

Finally, my wife Sissela read every word with meticulous
care and offered me many worthwhile suggestions. Much
of any value this book may have comes from all the help
I received from her and from my other good friends and
colleagues.

UNIVERSITIES IN THE MARKETPLACE

1 | THE ROOTS OF COMMERCIALIZATION

IT IS ONE OF THE UNWRITTEN, AND COMMONLY UNSPO-
KEN COMMONPLACES LYING AT THE ROOT OF MODERN
ACADEMIC POLICY THAT THE VARIOUS UNIVERSITIES
ARE COMPETITORS FOR THE TRAFFIC OF MERCHANT-
ABLE INSTRUCTION IN MUCH THE SAME FASHION AS RI-
VAL ESTABLISHMENTS IN THE RETAIL TRADE COMPETE
FOR CUSTOM.

—THORSTEIN VEBLEN

*The Higher Learning in America: A Memorandum on
the Conduct of Universities by Businessmen* (1918)

Toward the end of the twentieth century, American universities—with their stately buildings, tree-lined quadrangles,
and slightly disheveled, often-preoccupied professors—
found themselves in an enviable position. No longer quiet
enclaves removed from the busy world, they had emerged
as the nation's chief source for the three ingredients most
essential to continued growth and prosperity: highly trained
specialists, expert knowledge, and scientific advances others
could transform into valuable new products or life-saving
treatments and cures.

This newfound importance brought growing interest
from the media, increased funding from government agen-

cies and foundations, and closer scrutiny from public officials. It also brought abundant new opportunities to make
money. Universities learned that they could sell the right to
use their scientific discoveries to industry and find corporations willing to pay a tidy sum to sponsor courses delivered
by Internet or cable television. Apparel firms offered money
to have colleges place the corporate logo on their athletic
uniforms or, conversely, to put the university's name on
caps and sweatshirts sold to the public. Faculty members
began to bear such titles as Yahoo Professor of Computer
Science or K-Mart Professor of Marketing. The University
of Tennessee, in a coup of sorts, reportedly sold its school
color to a paint company hoping to find customers wishing
to share in the magic of the college's football team by daub-
ing their homes with "Tennessee Orange." One enterprising university even succeeded in finding advertisers willing
to pay for the right to place their signs above the urinals in
its men's rooms.

Commercial practices may have become more obvious,
but they are hardly a new phenomenon in American higher
education. By the early 1900s, the University of Chicago
was already advertising regularly to attract students, and the
University of Pennsylvania had established a "Bureau of
Publicity" to increase its visibility. In 1905, Harvard was
concerned enough about its profitable football team to hire
a 26-year-old coach at a salary equal to that of its president
and twice the amount paid to its full professors. As President Andrew Draper of the University of Illinois observed,
the university "is a business concern as well as a moral and
intellectual instrumentality, and if business methods are
not applied to its management, it will break down."[1]

What is new about today's commercial practices is not
their existence but their unprecedented size and scope. Be-

fore 1970, university presidents may have sounded like hucksters on occasion and resorted at times to advertising and other methods borrowed from the world of business. Nevertheless, commercialization in the strict sense of the term—that is, efforts to sell the work of universities for a profit—was largely confined to the periphery of campus life: to athletic programs and, in a few institutions, to correspondence schools and extension programs.* Today, opportunities to make money from intellectual work are pursued throughout the university by professors of computer science, biochemistry, corporate finance, and numerous other departments. Entrepreneurship is no longer the exclusive province of athletics departments and development offices; it has taken hold in science faculties, business schools, continuing education divisions, and other academic units across the campus.

What accounts for the growth of commercial activity in

*Some writers speak expansively of *commercialization* to include a wide range of behaviors and trends, notably (1) the influence of economic forces on universities (e.g., the growth of computer science majors and departments); (2) the influence of the surrounding corporate culture (e.g., the increased use on campuses of terms such as *CEO, bottom line,* or *brand name*); (3) the influence of student career interests on the curriculum (e.g., more vocational courses); (4) efforts to economize in university expenditures (hiring more adjunct teachers) or to use administrative methods adapted from business; or (5) attempts to quantify matters within the university that are not truly quantifiable, such as trying to express matters of value in monetary terms rather than qualitatively. Often, words such as *commercialization, corporatization,* or *commodification* are employed for rhetorical purposes to capitalize on the widespread distrust of business and business methods in academic circles. In view of the several meanings of *commercialization* and the motives with which the term is often used, it is especially important to be clear about one's own definition at the outset. To repeat, therefore, in this book *commercialization* is used to refer to efforts within the university to make a profit from teaching, research, and other campus activities.

institutions dedicated to higher learning? To Veblen, the obvious culprits were university presidents and their entourage of bureaucratic helpers. Intent upon accumulating money to expand the size and reputation of the institution, campus administrators were forever forcing the methods of the marketplace on a reluctant community of scholars. In Veblen's view, the remedy for the disease was as obvious as its cause: "The academic executive and all his works are an anathema and should be discontinued by the simple expedient of wiping him off the slate."[2]

If Veblen harbored any doubts about the reasons for commercialization, he did not acknowledge them. Even in his day, however, it should have been plain that the roots of the problem went beyond the academic bureaucracy. More than a few university presidents protested the growth of football programs, only to be overcome by the tidal force of enthusiastic students and alumni. Today, it is even more apparent that the recent surge in money-making activity on campus stems from causes far deeper than policies emanating from the president. University officials have surely initiated entrepreneurial ventures. But they often have little or nothing to do with the efforts of prominent professors to found their own companies, sell their services as teachers to corporations, or allow private companies to market their lectures through the Internet, tape, or videocassette. Nor is there any doubt that the greatest obstacles to reforming intercollegiate athletics continue to lie, not in the president's office, but among the alumni supporters, boosters, legislators, and others who insist on fielding winning teams.

If Veblen was wrong in heaping so much blame on university presidents, what else helps account for the recent burst of commercial activity on campus? Part of the explanation lies in the growing influence of the market throughout our society. Commercialization has plainly taken root, not only in higher education, but also in many other areas of American life and culture: health care, museums, public schools, even religion.[3] Entrepreneurial initiative, high executive salaries, and aggressive marketing techniques are all spreading to fields of endeavor quite outside the realm of business. Such practices set examples that legitimate the use of similar methods in universities. Nevertheless, merely noting the existence of a trend does not explain why it came about, let alone account for its sudden and deep penetration into an academic culture long considered an "ivory tower" set apart from the marketplace.

Several scholars have attributed the recent growth of money-making activity to a lack of purpose in the university.[4] Having lost sight of any clear mission beyond a vague commitment to "excellence," our sprawling multiversities are charged with creating a vacuum into which material pursuits have rushed in unimpeded. Explanations of this kind almost invariably come from philosophers, literary scholars, and other humanists. Although they talk expansively about the university, their background is chiefly in the humanities. Since these are the fields of study most widely accused of having lost their intellectual moorings, it is not surprising that their professors see a similar aimlessness as the cause of other ills that have overtaken the academy.

If one looks more broadly at the university, however, one quickly finds that many faculties and departments are quite clear about their purposes and that these are the very parts of the institution in which commercialization is most rampant. Within the traditional disciplines, no faculty members feel a stronger sense of mission than the scientists, yet it is there—not in the humanities—that commercialization has taken hold most firmly. Among the several faculties, none has a clearer sense of purpose than schools of business and medicine, yet it is their professors—not their colleagues in literature and philosophy—who are most deeply involved in lucrative consulting and entrepreneurial activity.

If there is an intellectual confusion in the academy that encourages commercialization, it is a confusion over means rather than ends. To keep profit-seeking within reasonable bounds, a university must have a clear sense of the values needed to pursue its goals with a high degree of quality and integrity. When the values become blurred and begin to lose their hold, the urge to make money quickly spreads throughout the institution. Just what these values are and how they are threatened by commercial pursuits are subjects discussed in subsequent chapters. For the moment, it is enough to say that loss of *purpose* is not a useful explanation for the recent growth of money-making ventures in the university.

Critics from the left have a different theory to explain the burgeoning commercial activity on campus. To them, such behavior is simply another illustration of the attempts by the businessmen and lawyers who sit on boards of trustees to "commodify" education and research, reduce the faculty to the status of employees, and ultimately, make the university serve the interests of corporate America.[5]

The influence of the private economy on the university is undeniable. Wealthy donors clearly alter the shape of the institution through the power of their benefactions. Anyone harboring doubts on this score need only contrast the opulence of business schools with the shabbiness of most schools of education and social work. The world of commerce and industry affects the curriculum in even more striking ways through the jobs it provides and the salaries it offers; witness the growth of undergraduate business majors, the rise of computer science departments, and the generous compensation offered to professors of management and economics, compared to that paid to colleagues in literature and philosophy.

It is one thing, however, to note the effects of the economy on academic institutions and quite another to imagine a plot on the part of business leaders to bend universities to their corporate purposes. It is true that toward the end of the nineteenth century, as American colleges transformed themselves into large research institutions, clergymen began to give way to business executives and lawyers on most university boards. Still, ascribing this trend to some sort of national corporate plot seems rather farfetched; there is a more benign explanation. As institutions of higher learning grew larger and more complicated, they needed trustees who could help them raise money and develop better methods of administration. Clergymen were poorly equipped for these tasks and were increasingly out of step, in any case, with faculties that were steadily becoming more secular and professional. Business executives and corporate lawyers simply seemed better suited to the changing needs of the university.

In the early years, some business-oriented trustees did try to impose their views on the institution, even to the point of firing faculty members with radical opinions. But professors soon organized to protest such interference. Eventually, board members had to modify their behavior and defer to scholarly judgments in academic matters or risk doing harm to the reputation of their university. Long before the recent wave of commercialization, therefore, trustees of major universities had become far less intrusive. By the 1960s, they were serving, as they do now, largely out of loyalty to their alma mater or from a sense of civic duty, rarely interfering with academic decisions except where necessary to guard the financial health of the institution. Today, if trustees encourage commercial ventures, they are far more likely to do so in order to find resources for the university's needs rather than to promote the selfish interests of American business.

Professors of higher education offer a different explanation for the growth of commercial activity on campus. In their view, the recent wave of entrepreneurial behavior is a response to the reductions in government support for higher education that began in the 1970s.[6] As the economy slowed after the energy crisis of 1973, Congress could no longer sustain the rapid increases in research funding that occurred during the 1950s and 1960s. State legislatures, burdened by the mounting costs of prisons, welfare, and health care for the indigent, followed suit and cut their appropriations for higher education, especially in the 1980s and 1990s. The result, according to this theory, was to force university officials and faculty members to look for new sources of funding. Eventually, enterprising presidents and entrepreneurial professors found ways to market their specialized knowledge and scientific discoveries in return for the cash they needed to make up for declining state support.

Government cutbacks may well be the precipitating cause that has led a number of universities in Britain, Australia, Scandinavia, and Holland to become more entrepreneurial.[7] In the United States, however, funding cuts are not the whole story. After all, the past two decades are hardly the first time that American higher education has experienced financial difficulties. Government funding slowed or declined in the early 1970s, not to mention the 1930s, yet universities did not respond with a burst of profit-seeking ventures.

Moreover, private universities in America have been no less entrepreneurial than their public counterparts even though few of them have had much state funding to lose, and most have seen their endowments surge during the heady stock market booms of the 1980s and 1990s. Basic biomedical scientists have been among the more enterprising in the academy, notwithstanding continued real increases in research support from the National Institutes of Health. Business schools and their faculties have pursued new money-making ventures with notable zeal despite having suffered few, if any, of the financial cutbacks that have beset other parts of the university. In short, declining appropriations may have played a part, but something more is surely required to explain the rise of entrepreneurial activity on American campuses during the last twenty years.

Universities share one characteristic with compulsive gamblers and exiled royalty: there is never enough money to satisfy their desires. Faculty and students are forever developing new interests and ambitions, most of which cost money. The prices of books and journals rise relentlessly. Better and more costly technology and scientific apparatus constantly appear and must be acquired to stay at the cutting edge. Presidents and deans are anxious to satisfy as many of these needs as they can, for their reputation depends on pleasing the faculty, preserving the standing of the institution, and building a legacy through the development of new programs.

The need for money, therefore, does not merely occur now and then in the wake of some ill-considered decision on the part of state officials to cut university budgets. It is a chronic condition of American universities, a condition inherent in the very nature of an institution forever competing for the best students and faculty. Such talented, ambitious people are constantly asking for more programs, more books, more equipment, more of everything required to satisfy their desire to pursue new interests and opportunities. In this sense, the recent surge of commercial activity is best understood as only the latest in a series of steps to acquire more resources, beginning with the use of aggressive marketing to attract tuition-paying students in the early twentieth century, and moving on to the determined search for government and foundation funding after World War II, and the increasingly sophisticated and intensive effort over the last fifty years to coax gifts from well-to-do alumni and other potential donors.*

What made commercialization so much more prevalent in American universities after 1980 was the rapid growth of opportunities to supply education, expert advice, and scientific knowledge in return for handsome sums of money. During the first half of the twentieth century, the chances to profit from such activities were not nearly so abundant. Executive education for business had not yet generated much interest. With very few exceptions (such as Harry Steenbock of the University of Wisconsin, who discovered how to enrich milk with vitamin *D*), academic scientists did not produce much research that had immediate commercial value. Outside of a few fields, such as chemistry and certain branches of engineering, corporations did not perceive much need to seek professorial advice.

---

*Each of these efforts has elicited its own corresponding criticism. Seeking out students produced charges of "consumerism." Soliciting government grants led to complaints in the late 1960s that universities were complicit in unsavory policies of the CIA and Defense Department. The launching of larger and larger capital drives has provoked concerns that university presidents are now being chosen primarily for their fundraising abilities.

The outlook for remunerative activity began to change after World War II. The contributions of science to the war effort convinced Washington policymakers to invest heavily in research, both in the natural sciences and, with the development of the National Institutes of Health, in medicine, as well. From 1948 to 1968, federal support for basic scientific research rose 25-fold in real dollars to reach almost $3 billion per year. The results exceeded expectations. Academic scientists helped develop the hydrogen bomb, launch satellites into space, and put a man on the moon. Advances in electrical engineering gave rise to civilian applications, most notably through the growth of electronics and the rise of the computer industry. The discovery of DNA and the development of gene-splicing techniques produced a revolution in medicine that helped launch a new biotechnology industry.

After three decades of large-scale federal support, priorities for basic science began to change. In the late 1970s, the slowdown in economic growth and the challenge of strong industrial competitors in Europe and Japan caused Congress to search for new ways to stimulate economic growth. As the Cold War waned, the emphasis of science policy in Washington shifted to place less weight on maintaining military superiority and more on ensuring America's competitiveness in the world economy.

This change in priorities led the government to consider new ways of linking university research to the needs of business. In 1980, Congress passed the Bayh-Dole Act, which made it much easier for universities to own and license patents on discoveries made through research paid for with public funds. Federal and state legislation offered subsidies for a variety of university-business cooperative ventures to help translate the fruits of academic science into new products and processes. Tax breaks encouraged industry to invest more in university-based science.

By all accounts, these initiatives achieved their purpose. Within a decade, two hundred universities had established offices to seek out commercially promising discoveries and patent them for licensing to companies. By the year 2000, universities had increased the volume of their patenting more than 10-fold and were earning more than $1 billion per year in royalties and license fees. Some twelve thousand academic scientists were participating in more than one thousand collaborative arrangements with local companies.[8] Many campuses had created centers to give technical assistance to small businesses or developed incubators offering seed money and advice to help entrepreneurs launch new enterprises. Several institutions formed special venture capital units to invest in companies founded by their professors.

Meanwhile, advances in genetics had suddenly made academic research commercially important to industry. Investors were willing to invest millions of dollars on the promise of a new idea without waiting for an actual product, let alone a healthy profit margin. New companies could be founded on the strength of a discovery in a university laboratory. Quickly, corporations doubled and redoubled their share of total academic research support, increasing it from 2.3 percent in the early 1970s to almost 8 percent by the year 2000.

Opportunities for profit also emerged after World War II in the field of adult education, as professionals in many fields felt the need to acquire new knowledge and to master new skills in order to prosper in an increasingly complex society. Extension schools attracted more students seeking to upgrade their vocational skills. Continuing education for doctors expanded greatly, as physicians scrambled to keep up with the rapid advances in medical science. Executive programs for business became increasingly popular, while corporate training of all kinds blossomed into a multibillion dollar per year activity.

The growth of money-making possibilities extended well beyond universities as institutions. Individual faculty members, especially in the best universities, found new ways to supplement their incomes with lucrative activities on the side. As biotechnology boomed, life scientists not only started to seek patents on their discoveries and take attractive consulting assignments; they also began to receive stock from new firms eager for their help and even to found new companies based on their own discoveries. Outside the sciences, business school professors traveled to corporations willing to pay substantial sums for days spent consulting or teaching their executives. Legal scholars began to collect large fees for advising law firms or their corporate clients. Economists, political scientists, psychologists, and many others discovered that their counsel was worth a tidy sum to companies, consulting firms, and other private organizations.

Even university administrators saw new possibilities for earning money outside the familiar realm of teaching and research. Alumni offices began organizing cruises, complete with lectures, to carry graduates to exotic places. Business offices started to license the use of the university's name on sweatshirts, mugs, and other paraphernalia. University museums built attractive shops to sell related bits of merchandise, and college bookstores moved off campus to downtown locations in search of greater profits.

Within a few short decades, therefore, a brave new world had emerged filled with attractive possibilities for turning specialized knowledge into money. University presidents, enterprising professors, and even administrative staff were all busy exploiting these opportunities.

Adding impetus to the search for money was a mounting competition among the nation's research universities. Institutional rivalry has always marked American higher education to a greater extent than in other countries. But several factors helped to intensify this tendency over the latter half of the twentieth century. Increases in the college-going population and a vast growth in federal funding and philanthropic aid helped to support a larger number of institutions with legitimate ambitions to become research universities of the first rank. Better transportation and increased financial aid permitted more students to consider a much wider range of institutions in deciding where to pursue their education. Meanwhile, state legislatures began to give more help to science and technology at their leading universities, hoping to boost their local economies by emulating the success achieved by Silicon Valley and Route 128 in Massachusetts. Even the advent of annual rankings by publications such as *U.S. News and World Report* may have played a part. Although every college president can recite the many weaknesses of these ratings, they do provide a highly visible index of success, and competition is always quickened by such measures, especially among institutions like universities whose work is too intangible to permit more reliable means of evaluation.

Increased competition in turn produced greater effort to find resources, because almost anything a university did to try to lift its reputation cost money: recruiting outstanding new professors, financing the merit scholarships to attract better students, and providing the salaries and facilities needed to keep respected faculty members from leaving for more welcoming venues. Increasingly, therefore, success in university administration came to mean being more resourceful than one's competitors in finding the funds to achieve new goals. Enterprising leaders seeking to improve their institution felt impelled to take full advantage of any legitimate opportunities that the commercial world had to offer.

Summing up, then, commercialization turns out to have multiple causes. Financial cutbacks undoubtedly acted as a spur to profit-seeking for some universities and some departments. The spirit of private enterprise and entrepreneurship that became so prominent in the 1980s helped encourage and legitimate such initiatives. A lack of clarity about academic values opened the door even wider. Keener competition gave still further impetus. But none of these stimuli would have borne such abundant fruit had it not been for the rapid growth of money-making opportunities provided by a more technologically sophisticated, knowledge-based economy.

What should one make of all the entrepreneurial activity that has ensued? Public officials intent on economic growth are undoubtedly pleased with the vigor universities have shown in placing their discoveries and expertise at the service of private industry. By all accounts, corporate investments in academic science have yielded a handsome return in new products and improved technology.[9] As a result, companies have increased their support, relieving the government of some of the burden of funding university research. Meanwhile, programs of continuing education have sprung up on campuses everywhere to satisfy the growing needs of professionals for further schooling at later points in their careers.

The new opportunities for earning money have clearly helped make universities more attentive to public needs. In

Europe as well as America, students of higher education have credited market forces with causing universities to become less stodgy and elitist and more vigorous in their efforts to aid economic growth.[10] Many people doubtless applaud this result and feel that universities are doing more to justify the large sums of public money governments spend on their behalf.

At the same time, the rise of entrepreneurial universities has not met with universal enthusiasm. Professors on the left complain about the "commodification" of higher education, claiming that universities have turned into "knowledge factories" where academic ideals are routinely compromised for the sake of money. According to sociologist Stanley Aronowitz, "the learning enterprise has become subject to the growing power of administration, which more and more responds not to faculty and students, except at the margins, but to political and market forces that claim sovereignty over higher education."[11] To cultural anthropologist Wesley Shumar, learning and research have "come to be valued in terms of their ability to be translated into cash or merchandise and not in any other ways, such as aesthetic or recreational pleasure. Eventually, the idea that there are other kinds of value is lost."[12]

Most critics do not paint the current situation in quite such bleak colors. But many are afraid that commercially oriented activities will come to overshadow other intellectual values and that university programs will be judged primarily by the money they bring in and not by their intrinsic intellectual quality. They view with dismay how the surrounding economy draws more and more students into vocational fields of study, elevates the salaries of computer scientists, business school professors, and others whose work relates to business, and attracts ever greater sums of outside money for subjects of commercial relevance to the neglect of other worthy, but less practical, fields of study. Even those who support the university's efforts to aid economic growth worry about the side effects of profit-seeking and the unseemliness of institutions of learning hawking everything from sweatshirts to adult education.

These concerns are linked to a broader disquiet over the encroachments of the marketplace on the work of hospitals, cultural institutions, and other areas of society that have traditionally been thought to serve other values. Almost everyone concedes that competitive markets are effective in mobilizing the energies of participants to satisfy common desires. And yet the apprehensions remain. However hard it is to explain these fears, they persist as a mute reminder that something of irreplaceable value may get lost in the relentless growth of commercialization.

2 | AVOIDING BIAS

Commercialization is not a neutral word, let alone a term of approval, in most academic circles. Rarely, if ever, does one read that a university's efforts to "commercialize" its educational programs or its research activities have met with applause from its students or enthusiasm from its faculty. On the contrary, to commercialize a university is to engage in practices widely regarded in the academy as suspect, if not downright disreputable.

These reactions are neither recent nor surprising. Scholars, especially in the traditional disciplines, have deliberately chosen academic life in preference to the ways of commerce, in part because they look upon the search for truth and knowledge as a worthier calling than the quest for material wealth. Skeptical about the motives of company executives and doubtful whether "captains of industry" can fully appreciate the ends of learning and research, professors have long worried about the influence of businessmen-trustees and the use of corporate methods in campus administration. Veblen spoke for many of his colleagues when he warned in 1918 that "the ideals of scholarship are yielding ground, in an uncertain and varying degree before the pressure of businesslike exigencies."[1] His famous polemic against university administrators, *The Higher Learning in America*, bore the subtitle, *A Memorandum on the Conduct of Universities by Businessmen*. Even the birth of business schools early in the last century met with much suspicion on American campuses. Abraham Flexner, the leading authority of his day on higher education, scolded Harvard for merely creating such a school, arguing that business was not a true profession and did not require the mental discipline, the noble purposes, or the store of specialized knowledge deserving of a university education.[2]

Members of the university who resist commercial influences have several concerns. They fear that money and efficiency may gradually come to have too dominant a place in academic decision making and that the verdict of the market will supplant the judgment of scholars in deciding what to teach and whom to appoint. They suspect that commercialization and those who favor it will strengthen the forces that look at teaching and research chiefly as means to some practical end rather than as ends in themselves. Most of all, they worry that business methods, with their emphasis on accountability and control, may encroach upon the exceptional personal freedom that is such a cherished part of academic life.

Such concerns have long given rise to a suspicion of academic administrators and a fear that they are taking over the university with their alien corporate ways. As early as 1909, Harvard alumnus John Jay Chapman complained that "the men who control Harvard today are very little else than businessmen, running a large department store which dispenses education to the millions."[3] Sixty years later, Peter Caws remarked that "trustees, presidents, deans, registrars, secretaries, janitors, and the like are not, strictly speaking, part of the university at all. . . . They are ancillary to the real business of the university, and only the supplanting of the community model by the corporation model has put them in their present dominant position."[4] More recently still, sociologist Stanley Aronowitz observed disapprovingly that "the learning enterprise has become subject to the growing power of administration, which more and more responds not to faculty and students but to political and corporate forces that claim sovereignty over higher education."[5]

These critics may use harsher words than most of their faculty colleagues. Still, the underlying concerns are widely shared. Through the years, the most common criticisms heard on campus about university leaders have been that they are enlarging the bureaucracy and "trying to run the university like General Motors." Such complaints have not stopped presidents from employing business consultants to review their operations or from talking grandly to alumni on occasion about "Total Quality Management," "reinvention," "restructuring," and other terms borrowed from the corporate lexicon. But language of this kind invariably grates on the academic mind and threatens to widen the gulf between faculty and administration.

THE RELEVANCE OF BUSINESS

If every business practice were truly at odds with the ideal university, there would be good reason to resist the growth of commercialization. But is the world of business as alien to the affairs of academic institutions as many scholars seem to think? Before writing companies off as irrelevant, those who care for higher education should ask themselves whether the corporate sector could have some valuable lessons to offer universities.

Corporations, after all, seem very successful at carrying out the functions society has assigned them. No other form of organization—government-owned factories, collective farms, cooperatives, or what you will—has done as well at mobilizing capital to produce the goods and services people want at reasonable prices. Granted, private enterprise is not perfect. Some firms gain too much market power and charge excessive prices; some corporate executives cheat and break the law to get ahead; some businesses take advantage of the ignorance of their customers or exploit the weakness of their employees. Still, the private corporation— guided by the marketplace, stimulated by competition, and regulated by government—seems to possess a set of incentives that drive its members to do remarkably well in responding to the desires of consumers and achieving high levels of productive efficiency.

In contrast, the university strikes many critics as a kind of anarchy, ill-suited for any purpose other than securing the comfort and convenience of the tenured professors. Officials of the university have very little authority over their senior faculty. The latter have virtually complete license to do as they choose, thanks to the security of tenure buttressed by the safeguards of academic freedom. Since it is difficult to monitor closely the work of highly educated professionals, faculty members can travel more than the university rules allow or remain at home most of the day tending their garden or enjoying their hobbies without much fear of detection. So long as they meet their scheduled classes and refrain from criminal acts or other grossly improper behavior, they can stay happily in their jobs until they retire.

Despite these apparent weaknesses, American research universities have also been unusually successful in carrying out their appointed tasks. In the eyes of most informed observers, here and abroad, they are the best in the world at what they do. Their preeminence may seem surprising in view of their loose, anarchic structure. Yet research universities turn out to have a web of incentives subtler than those in more hierarchical institutions, but effective nonetheless for carrying out most of their basic functions and responsibilities.

In the case of science and scholarship, for example, a tenured professor may never publish anything and still keep his job. But few professors ever receive tenure in a major university unless they are strongly motivated to work hard at their research. The sheer satisfaction of arriving at a novel idea, discovering a secret of nature, or crafting a well-constructed article or book gives a powerful incentive to sustain their interest and dedication. Success brings further rewards in the form of prizes, job offers, salary increases, invitations to conferences, and other signs of recognition. In many disciplines, especially the sciences, research requires outside grants, which in turn depend on the continued ability to win approval for one's projects from qualified peers. Last, but far from least, there is the fear of being regarded as inconsequential by one's colleagues, one's students, or, even worse, by oneself. Together, these pressures constitute a formidable set of stimuli, driving the typical professor in a research university to go to great lengths to succeed as a scientist or scholar.

Another set of incentives causes professors to work hard at the critical task of evaluating and selecting candidates to serve as junior faculty members or tenured colleagues. Conscientious people, of course, are naturally inclined to pay close attention to matters of such concern to fellow scholars being considered for appointment. In addition, faculty members have a strong personal interest in keeping up the reputation of the academic unit to which they belong. Membership in a highly regarded department adds to one's own reputation and helps attract able graduate students with whom to work. Making first-rate appointments also enlivens the intellectual community in which one lives and works. It is true that faculty politics, favoritism, and gender discrimination will sometimes enter into deliberations over appointments and promotions. On the whole, however, professors who serve on search committees or on panels to review promotions spend remarkable amounts of time studying the writings of prospective appointees and discussing their merits with other members of the faculty.

Finally, the keen competition for applicants among rival colleges and universities creates a powerful incentive for each institution to try to match or exceed its rivals in providing students with programs, services, and facilities of every kind. No country boasts such an array of academic opportunities to suit every vocational or intellectual purpose. No country offers undergraduates such a wealth of student services and extracurricular activities. From computers to gymnasia to huge catalogues stuffed with courses, American universities vie with each other to meet virtually every legitimate desire that able young people can express. Critics may claim that the resulting competition leads to excessive duplication of programs or to unnecessary services and amenities for undergraduates, but no one can deny that university officials are highly motivated to attract students by responding to their needs.

Contrary to popular impressions, then, research universities have a network of incentives that serve quite well to inspire presidents, deans, and professors to work hard at most of their appointed tasks. But the incentives are not perfect. On three important counts, the environment in most research universities does not do enough to encourage the behaviors needed for the sake of the students, the society, and the well-being of the institution itself. In these respects, at least, it is conceivable that universities have something to learn from the world of commercial enterprise.

In the first place, university administrators do not have as strong an incentive as most business executives to lower costs and achieve greater efficiency. To be sure, academic leaders want to eliminate waste. Every dollar saved from building maintenance or personnel administration is a dollar more for education and research. Since deans and presidents are under constant pressure to meet demands for new academic programs and added faculty and facilities, they are naturally anxious not to squander scarce resources on administrative or support services. Still, there are several reasons for suspecting that university officials will be less successful than business executives in operating efficiently. Presidents and deans lack the experience of most corporate managers in administering large organizations. Because the principal purposes of their universities are academic, they must be intellectual leaders more than administrators. For this reason, their backgrounds and training are almost always in research and teaching rather than administration. Once in office, their success is measured much more by their accomplishments in building academic programs than by their record in achieving greater efficiency. They cannot win huge bonuses by cutting costs; indeed, the ethos of the university keeps them from earning sums remotely comparable to those of top business leaders. Finally, though cost savings are helpful to universities, they are rarely a matter of life and death. No research university has ever ceased to exist because of inefficiency. In constrast, losing one's job for poor performance, being taken over by corporate raiders, and going bankrupt under pressure from more efficient rivals are ever-present possibilities for most company executives. Like the threat of imminent execution, the fear of extinction works famously to concentrate the mind.

The point of these comparisons is not that universities should give massive bonuses to reward their presidents, still less that major research institutions should be allowed to go bankrupt periodically. Rather, the moral of the story is simply that corporations have long had powerful reasons to work especially hard at operating efficiently and that universities may consequently have something to learn from their experience. True, seeking cost savings in teaching and research is a hazardous undertaking that can do more harm than good, as we will discover in a moment. Even so, every major university spends hundreds of millions of dollars each year on such business-like functions as food service, building maintenance, construction, and personnel. In these domains, certainly, corporate practice and experience may have valuable lessons to teach.

A second important lesson universities can learn from business is the value of striving continuously to improve the quality of what they do. Because of the growing speed of innovation and change, businesses have been trying particularly hard in recent years to transform their organizations so that they can learn and adapt more quickly. In today's world, as former Shell executive Arie de Geus has remarked, "the ability to learn faster than your competitor may be the only sustainable source of competitive advantage."[6] To excel in this way, corporate executives have made major efforts to decentralize their organizations and give more discretion to semi-autonomous groups to experiment and innovate.

Universities, too, need to learn and adapt more quickly, but they have succeeded only partially. Faculties do work hard at improving their research. Unfortunately, the same cannot be said of their teaching and educational programs. Take almost any product—automobiles, computers, television sets, and so forth—and compare the improvement over the past twenty-five years with the progress in the quality of college instruction. Most commercial products are distinctly superior to what they were a quarter century ago. In contrast, most college teaching remains, with a few technological embellishments, very much as it was twenty-five years ago—or even fifty years ago, for that matter.

Some faculty members will cry foul, claiming that teaching is simply not comparable to a piece of merchandise. But protestations of this kind cannot hide the fact that very few universities make a serious, systematic effort to study their own teaching, let alone try to assess how much their students learn or to experiment with new methods of instruction. Instead, faculty members invoke all manner of rationalizations—academic freedom, professional autonomy, privacy—to resist efforts to subject their teaching to outside scrutiny.

Some years ago, an instructor at the University of California, Berkeley, Uri Treisman, broke with this tradition by trying to discover why African-American students in his calculus course performed so much more poorly than their Asian-American classmates. He quickly found that the two groups studied in very different ways. While Asian-Americans worked together, African-Americans studied alone. As a result, when an Asian-American student had difficulty understanding a problem, other students were at hand to help her over her difficulty. In contrast, African-American students who were stymied lacked any comparable peer support and tended to become discouraged and to fall further and further behind. Unlike most other instructors, Treisman proceeded to test his observation by persuading a sample of African-Americans to study in groups. The results were striking. When African-American students worked together, not only did their calculus grades improve markedly; they were more likely than the other African-Americans to finish the course, remain as science majors, and graduate from college.[7]

What happened next tells much about attitudes within the academy toward efforts to examine teaching and learning to discover how they can be improved. If researchers had made a discovery of this kind on a problem of scientific interest, investigators around the country would have reacted quickly by trying to replicate the findings and to discover whether the effects of studying in groups carried over into other fields besides calculus. In Treisman's case, however, though it is believed that significant group effects occur only in some subjects and not others, no such response took place. As a result, though Treisman's methods have spread to other campuses, no one yet knows exactly when group studying improves learning and when it does not.

Many faculty members will not like to admit that anything as crass as money could be needed to induce professors to work harder at teaching their students. It is more comforting to think that the desire for truth and respect for learning offer motivation enough. Nevertheless, the record shows that the typical campus environment fails to inspire the faculty to do all they should to meet the needs of their students. While every research university has a number of dedicated teachers, none can claim that nearly all of its professors work consistently hard at their teaching. Studies abound on the effectiveness of various technologies and innovations to improve instruction, but few faculty members have studied this literature, and even fewer universities make a comprehensive effort to use the findings to enhance the quality of teaching on their campus. It is at least worth considering, therefore, whether the profit motive might provide the incentive needed to break through this wall of inertia.

Recent history has also shown that business methods and incentives can have a useful role to play even in the cherished domain of academic research. For decades, the federal government has been contributing billions of dollars each year to support university research. Although the public doubtless derives much pride and satisfaction from the advances scientists have made in pushing back the boundaries of knowledge, no one doubts that the dominant motive for giving all this money is to finance discoveries that will someday lead to useful new products, successful medical treatments, and labor-saving technologies. Yet prior to 1980, when Congress passed the Bayh-Dole Act, few universities could pretend that they were making much effort to review the work in their laboratories for advances that could be put to practical use. Only when Congress expanded their rights to seek patents and collect royalties for their discoveries did campus administrators mount a serious effort to help the public gain a greater return on the billions of tax dollars invested in academic research. In this case, then, the profit motive proved decisive in causing universities to fulfill their responsibility to serve the public.

The point of these remarks is simple. Left to itself, the contemporary research university does not contain sufficient incentives to elicit all of the behaviors that society has a right to expect. In some respects, corporations, moved by pecuniary incentives, do a better job than universities of carrying out the tasks society has given them. The motives that inspire professors may be nobler than those that animate corporate leaders, but in some respects, at least, they have proved less effective. Professors who look down on business would do well to bear this point in mind before dismissing the ways of commerce as irrelevant to the academy.

LIMITS TO THE RELEVANCE OF BUSINESS

Although skepticism and resistance have traditionally been the most prevalent feelings toward business on most university campuses, plenty of professors respect the accomplishments of corporate leaders and admire the way the market works to shape human behavior. Such sentiments have long been especially common in faculties of management. In recent decades, they have also gained ground in social science departments and law schools where many professors now regard competitive markets as the most effective means of ordering human behavior, not just in business, but in politics, law, medicine, and other spheres of activity. In view of these trends, it is only prudent to balance the preceding discussion by noting the limitations of corporate methods and market models as guides for university administration.

As many critics have pointed out, whatever value consumer demand may have in deciding what goods to produce, it is not a reliable guide for choosing an appropriate curriculum or constructing an ideal research agenda. Some scientific problems are well worth investigating although they have no foreseeable commercial value, while other fields, such as Egyptology or epistemology, are deserving of first-rate scholarship even though few people care to read about them. Subjects such as Russian literature or moral philosophy are valued parts of the curriculum even if they are not appreciated by many undergraduates or especially useful in finding a job. Thus, no responsible educator will build a faculty or construct a curriculum simply by hiring the professors and providing the courses that will allow students to study whatever they please.*

Leading a university is also a much more uncertain and ambiguous enterprise than managing a company because the market for higher education lacks tangible measureable goals by which to measure success. Academic leaders cannot look to precise indicators comparable to market share, return on investment, stock prices, or cost per unit of production to determine how well their institution is progressing. No university can measure the value of its research output or determine reliably how much its students are learning. For this reason, efforts to adapt the corporate model by trying to measure performance or "manage by objective" are much more difficult and dangerous for universities than they are for commercial enterprises.

Ignoring this problem, some state governments have been trying to make universities more accountable by basing a portion of their funding on quantitative measures, such as improvements in standardized test scores or increases in the volume of government research grants.[6] Measures of this kind, however, are far too crude for making sound budgetary decisions. Larger government grants may have nothing to do with improvements in the quality of the university's research, but may simply result from an increase in the federal research budget or a shift in priorities

---

*This is not to say that university faculties, left to themselves, always do a good job of choosing an appropriate curriculum. American universities, after all, neglected coursework in practical ethics almost completely for several decades. Their Arts and Sciences faculties currently display scant interest in preparing undergraduates to be democratic citizens, a task once regarded as the principal purpose of a liberal education and one urgently needed at this moment in the United States.

to favor fields that happen to be well represented at the university. Similarly, standardized tests provide a crude approximation at best of what college students should be learning. As a result, efforts to base state funding on changes in test scores will either be ignored by professors or cause them to waste time teaching less important things and coaching students to answer multiple-choice questions.

Universities must likewise be cautious in looking to corporate models to achieve greater efficiency in their operations. Business methods can offer useful clues for cutting expenditures on building maintenance or support services. But efficiency is not a very helpful guide for teaching and research. A corporate trustee will periodically make news by calling for greater productivity through heavier teaching loads and fewer faculty members per student, but such measures can easily damage the quality of education. Similarly, an efficiency expert can identify redundant positions in science departments, but eliminating the positions may gravely diminish the value of the research effort. As James Watson is said to have remarked: "To encourage real creativity, you need to have a good deal of slack."

Maximizing profit falls equally short as a proper guide for making decisions in a university. The best-known colleges could charge a great deal more than they currently do and still attract a student body perfectly capable of graduating with respectable grades. Yet few people would be pleased with such a policy. Most would agree that opportunities to attend a selective college should be awarded insofar as possible, not by students' ability to pay, but according to "merit," a much mooted term that includes the intellectual capacities of the applicants, their potential to fulfill the needs of society in later life, and their ability to contribute to the understanding of their fellow students. Similarly, many faculties could probably design courses to lower their cost without having to cut tuition, but few would defend such a policy or argue that it will necessarily benefit either the public or the students.

THE CHALLENGE

In sum, the ways of the marketplace are neither consistently useful nor wholly irrelevant in trying to improve the performance of research universities. That is what makes the problem of commercialization difficult. Educators must use their own judgment in deciding when to pursue opportunities for profit or adopt other business practices.* This is often hard to do when outside critics urge academic leaders to copy corporations, while sentiments within the academy resist anything that smacks of commercial methods and values. Caught between these conflicting pressures, university officials can easily become confused. How can they decide when to heed the call of the marketplace and when to refuse its allure?

The most obvious way to proceed is to weigh the advantages and disadvantages of each commercial opportunity. How much revenue is the university likely to receive if it acts affirmatively? What risks will it run, what costs might it incur, and do these disadvantages outweigh the tangible rewards of going forward?

This approach seems straightforward and sensible, but

---

*The emphasis throughout is on the dilemmas of commercialization for the university and the appropriate response to promote the purposes and protect the values of the institution. The ethical problems that faculty members encounter in pursuing lucrative outside opportunities are not a concern of this book, except insofar as the activities and ties of individual professors threaten the interests and values of their university.

where will it lead the university? What if Nike offers Yale a hefty sum in exchange for the right to place large advertisements on the walls of every classroom? What if the McKinsey consulting firm promises to endow a Wharton School executive program in return for the right to make a brief pitch about its services at the beginning of the first class and to include a company brochure in the materials distributed to every student on arrival? Or suppose that some well-meaning trustee, like the financier in my dream, urges Stanford to capitalize on the thousands of talented applicants it attracts every year by auctioning off the last one hundred places in the class. In each of these cases, the benefits are very tangible, while the costs seem speculative and hard to specify. Even so, most people, inside universities and out, would shrink from accepting any of the three propositions.

"This is all very obvious," some readers will respond. "For example, if Stanford auctioned off one hundred places in the entering class, it would be sacrificing something essential to its basic mission—the intellectual quality of its student body." But the problem is not as simple as that. Decisions about which applicants to admit are notoriously imperfect, and the best available indicators, such as SAT scores, are very crude predictors of academic performance, let alone success in later life. A university could easily construct a successful auction limited to students with good enough test scores that their admission would not cause any demonstrable loss of quality. If part of the proceeds were allocated to merit scholarships, freshman scores might even improve, leaving a tidy profit for other university purposes.

In short, simple cost-benefit analysis will often fail to yield clear answers about how universities should respond to tempting commercial opportunities. The intellectual difficulties make it all the more necessary to guard against deep-seated biases either for or against corporations and market-based solutions. How to decide what to do remains a puzzle that later chapters of this book will attempt to solve. To prepare for the task, however, we need to look more closely at the several fields in which commercial opportunities have arisen and ask whether experience has anything to teach that will aid us in our search.

3 | ATHLETICS

On a sunny afternoon in 1852, two groups of oarsmen—
one from Harvard, one from Yale—raced against each
other on Lake Winnipesaukee. The students may not have
known it, but they were participating in the first intercollegiate sports contest in the United States. Even then, although there were no paying spectators and no television
crews, the event had definite commercial overtones. The
race was the brainchild of a railroad owner and real estate
developer who hoped to attract the public's attention to
the charms of Southern New Hampshire by staging an
athletic spectacle. With calculating shrewdness, he lured
the athletes to compete by offering to pay all their expenses and supply them with "lavish prizes" and "unlim-
ited alcohol."

From this modest beginning, intercollegiate athletics, especially football and basketball, have become big business
on many campuses, attracting large audiences and generat-
ing millions of dollars in revenue every year. In one sense,
of course, they are a special case, affecting a small number
of students and a set of activities quite separate from the
central mission of education and research. Yet athletics, as
practiced by most major universities, are the oldest form of
commercialization in American higher education. As such,
they have important lessons to teach about attempts to

make money from campus activity and the perils they hold for even the most eminent institutions.

College sports grew rapidly after the Civil War. By the end of the nineteenth century, most of the trappings of big-time athletic programs were already visible: professional coaches, training tables, admission charges, paid recruiters, and scholarships for promising athletes.[1] Winning was all-important. William Rainey Harper, President of the University of Chicago, hired the legend-to-be, Amos Alonzo Stagg, as his first football coach, instructing him to "develop teams which we can send around the country and knock out all the colleges."[2] In those wide-open days, some schools were not above using traveling mercenaries to improve their chances. In their eagerness to win, they resorted to "dressing up the butcher's boy, the iron molder, the boiler maker, or even a bond salesman in football clothing."[3] Students and alumni loved it. In the 1890s, 40,000 people watched a championship game in New York City. "Jam-packed college grandstands went wild rooting for 'heroes' who attended school only during baseball and football seasons."[4]

The football played in the early years of the twentieth century was even more violent than it is today. Observers recall watching team members "jumping on downed players with their knees, while striking with closed fists."[5] New formations such as the "flying wedge" wreaked havoc, resulting in twenty-one deaths in 1904 alone. One year later, President Theodore Roosevelt called a meeting of college presidents at the White House to consider ways of stopping the mayhem. Out of such concerns, what is now the National Collegiate Athletic Association (NCAA) was born in 1906 to develop uniform rules to guide college sports.

As intercollegiate football became more savage, some

college presidents took a public stand against it. At Harvard, President Charles W. Eliot tried to abolish the sport on the ground that it had "become a brutal, cheating, demoralizing game," but he was overruled by his governing boards.[6] In addition to being popular with students and alumni, football generated publicity that was widely believed to help colleges compete for students, thus endearing the sport to many trustees. According to Henry Pritchett, writing in 1911, those few presidents who tried to stand up for "sound educational goals" were often dismissed "because of the popular cry for greater numbers [of students] or winning athletic teams."[7]

As football and other intercollegiate sports tightened their grip on American colleges, the quest for revenue grew more and more determined. Universities built bigger stadia to attract larger paying audiences. Gradually, students were moved further and further away from the 50-yard line to make room for "boosters" who contributed money to the athletic program. Later, athletic departments added luxury boxes to lure corporate sponsors and other wealthy patrons who could afford to pay large sums for privileged accommodations complete with food and bar service. Radio, and then television, brought increasingly lucrative contracts for the benefit of colleges with teams good enough to command a national audience. Universities negotiated agreements with apparel manufacturers Adidas, Nike, and Reebok to obtain free equipment and cash in return for having their athletes wear the corporate insignia during athletic contests. Bowl games multiplied, producing additional television revenue: over $10 million for teams fortunate enough to win an invitation to one of the premier postseason contests. Meanwhile, the annual "March Madness" basketball playoffs came to enjoy even greater success, attracting such large audiences that the NCAA negotiated an exclusive 11-year contract with CBS for the princely sum of $6 billion.

THE CHIMERA OF PROFITABILITY

As revenues mounted, colleges, to their chagrin, quickly learned that it took a lot of money to make money. Developing high-profile, winning teams required high-priced coaches. In 2001, the Knight Commission (a collection of notables convened to try to reform college sports) reported that roughly thirty football and basketball coaches were earning more than $1 million per year, a sum several times that of most college presidents.[8] Coaching staffs gradually grew in size to give more specialized, personal instruction to athletes. All-weather practice fields became de rigueur for serious football programs, along with weight rooms with trainers where athletes could engage in year-round conditioning and bodybuilding. As Virginia Tech Athletic Director Jim Weaver described it, "If you are not upgrading your facilities, you are going backward."[9]

The mounting costs of maintaining a competitive athletic program have made it difficult for universities to achieve real financial success from major sports. Although many Division I schools claim to make money on their football and basketball programs, many do not, especially if the capital costs of their facilities are accurately counted.[10] Only a handful of universities, such as Florida State and Notre Dame—perhaps no more than ten to twenty in all—make a profit on their entire athletic program, since the NCAA requires institutions with Division IA (big-time) status to field a minimum number of fourteen teams, few of which can attract enough spectators or television interest to break even. Institutions such as the University of Buffalo, which have tried moving up to Division IA, have typically ended by losing substantial sums.

The resulting situation has been aptly described by former NCAA President Walter Byers: "Money begets money, but in college athletics, there never seems to be enough of it. Traditional net revenue producers—for instance, Notre Dame, Penn State, Michigan, and Nebraska—continually set higher expenditure levels that destroy the balance sheets of most of the other Division IA colleges that are trying to keep up."[11] After reviewing the evidence, James Shulman and William Bowen tersely remarked in the course of their detailed empirical study of college sports: "As a money-making venture, athletics is a bad business."[12]

The imperatives of big-time intercollegiate athletics invite corruption. Coaches are under intense pressure to win in order to keep their jobs. So are athletic directors, who have to fill the stands and attract television coverage to gain the revenue they need to meet the heavy cost of the program. Admissions offices are importuned to accept student athletes with academic credentials far below the norm. Everyone involved must do their part to enroll the outstanding athletes so essential to success on the field and at the box office. Small wonder that coaches are repeatedly accused of trying to lure star prospects with offers of money "under the table" or that scandals periodically erupt involving changing grades, cheating on exams, or even altering transcripts to make talented athletes admissible and keep them eligible to play.

TRYING TO KEEP ORDER

The NCAA has the thankless task of making and enforcing rules to keep athletic programs honest. Until 1948, however, the organization had no real enforcement power. As a result, although it outlawed all athletic scholarships and other financial subsidies for athletes, the rule was so widely disregarded that it was finally repealed. After enforcement mechanisms were added in 1948, the history of the organization became a saga of repeated attempts to pass rules followed by increasingly sophisticated efforts to get around them. As the president of New Mexico State observed, "the NCAA can plug one hole, but someone'll go and drill another."[13]

Year by year, the rulebook has grown in size to consume hundreds of pages. Cheating on the part of coaches, athletic directors, alumni, and other boosters has grown along with it. No one really knows just how often the rules are broken. During the 1980s, however, more than half of the Division IA universities were censured, sanctioned, or put on probation by the NCAA for breaking its rules.[14] According to one professional player's agent, "everyone is being paid and signed. If anyone says otherwise, they're really stupid, blind, or they're lying."[15] Although college officials make periodic efforts to improve the system, long-time NCAA leader, Walter Byers, reports that "college athletics reform movements spanning almost 90 years have been remarkably consistent. They never reformed much of anything."[16]

Fortunately, the pressures and petty corruptions of big-time college athletics have not spread full-blown to all institutions. The many colleges that make up the NCAA's Division III allow no athletic scholarships and do not try to make money from their programs. Several large universities, such as the University of Chicago, Johns Hopkins, MIT, and Washington of St. Louis, have deliberately de-emphasized sports to a point that the risk of serious wrongdoing is negligible. Some other well-known institutions, such as those of the Ivy League, retain a vigorous intercollegiate program but have regulated themselves fairly strictly, albeit at a substantial cost to the quality of their teams and the revenue they generate.

Notwithstanding these many exceptions, well over one hundred institutions, including almost all of the major public universities, do engage in high-pressure intercollegiate athletics to an extent that seriously conflicts with academic principles. Most of the rest will bend their normal standards to some extent in order to win on the playing field, or at least keep up with the competition. Even small liberal arts colleges admit substantial numbers of applicants each year "on recommendation of the coaches," a sign that many students are being admitted who would not have gained entry were it not for their athletic skills. Meanwhile, the cost of intercollegiate athletics dwarfs the amounts made available for community service, student orchestras, theater, and other worthwhile extracurricular activities.

THE ACADEMIC COSTS

The most obvious cost of a successful revenue-producing program is the sacrifice of normal admissions standards. According to data for the class of 1993, collected by James Shulman and William Bowen, members of the football and basketball teams in selective public universities such as Penn State and Michigan had combined SAT scores averaging 237 points below the mean for the class as a whole.[17] In Division IA private universities, such as Duke and Stanford, the gap was even greater, reaching 307 for basketball players and 292 for members of the football team.[18] At almost all the big-time schools, and even at many Division II and III schools, the differences have gradually widened over the years.*[19]

As one might expect from their lower SAT scores, athletes tend to perform less well academically than their classmates, especially at Division IA schools, and the differences have steadily increased. According to Shulman and Bowen, the average Division IA male athlete entering college in 1951 finished at the 48th percentile of his class, very close to the average for the entire student body.[20] Twenty-five years later, the performance of male athletes had slipped to the 40th percentile, only to slip again to the 34th percentile for the class matriculating in 1989. (Male athletes in high-profile sports did even worse, only reaching the 25th percentile for the class entering in 1989.[21])

These results are not merely a consequence of admitting athletes with poor academic credentials. In all types of selective colleges, except in Division IA public universities, male athletes in high-profile and even in minor sports tend to receive substantially lower grades than one would have predicted from their high school record and SAT scores.†[22]

---

*In most of the so-called "minor" sports, which do not make money, gaps in test scores are much less pronounced at Division IA schools and have not grown appreciably, although they exceed one hundred points in wrestling, basketball, tennis, and several other sports. Gaps of one hundred points also exist in wrestling and tennis at Ivy League schools and even at small liberal arts colleges, though these differences, too, do not seem to be growing. See James L. Shulman and William G. Bowen, *The Game of Life: College Sports and Educational Values* (2001), p. 357.

†Fortunately, the gap between women athletes and their classmates is considerably smaller than that of men both in SATs and academic performance. Only in Division IA schools, where women's basketball is coming more and more to resemble its high-pressure male counterpart, have the differences in SAT scores between female athletes and their classmates grown substantially. Overall, the academic rank of women athletes at every type of school stood above the 40th percentile of the class for students entering in 1989.

The reasons for this disappointing performance are not well understood. One plausible explanation, however, is that most college athletes today are heavily recruited, choose their college for its athletic rather than its academic program, and continue to be far more absorbed by their sport than by the subjects being taught in their courses. For them, classwork is a distraction from the real business of winning on the athletic field.

Graduation rates are also lower than they should be for male athletes in major revenue-making programs. By the late 1990s, according to the Knight Commission, only 34 percent of basketball players and 48 percent of football players received a degree within six years from Division IA colleges.[23] These figures are not markedly lower than those of other students. Still, they are troubling because almost all of these athletes get full scholarships (and hence have little likelihood of dropping out for financial reasons), not to mention extensive tutoring to help them through their coursework. Moreover, although other students often transfer to other schools and eventually graduate, athletes cannot do so without losing a year's eligibility. Thus, football and basketball players are less likely than their classmates to receive a B.A. even though they have special advantages that should boost their chances to earn a degree.

The pressure to win in big-time programs also helps to create a unique culture for recruited athletes that gives them a different, more impoverished educational experience than that of their classmates. Much of their day during the season is spent practicing or traveling to games away from the campus. The time required by their sport, including working out during the off-season, makes it difficult for them to take challenging courses or to engage in the extracurricular activities enjoyed by their classmates.[24] In many schools, they take most of their classes in majors, such as sports management, that are rarely equal in academic rigor to the normal run of courses in the college.

Fred Akers, former football coach at the University of Texas, describes the prevailing philosophy of Division I sports programs. "Most coaches believe that the best way to win is to put their players in the most intense training possible, keep at 'em from dawn to dusk and into the night."[25] The undergraduate experience of athletes, therefore, has become something quite unlike that of their fellow students. As the football coach at Iowa State allegedly told a *Sports Illustrated* reporter, "Not more than 20 percent of the football players go to college for an education. And that may be a high figure."[26] Many coaches do not want to have their athletes too distracted by coursework. Sonny Randle, when he coached the University of Virginia football team, is reported to have said: "We've stopped recruiting young men who want to come here to be students first and athletes second."[27]

In short, high-pressure athletics immerse students so completely in their sport that they cannot easily obtain the normal educational benefits of attending college, even if they manage to graduate. As one Tulsa University basketball player put it: "In college the coaches be a lot more concerned about winning and the money comin' in. If they don't win, they may get the boot, and so they pass the pressure onto us athletes. . . . I go to bed every night I be thinkin' about basketball. That's what college athaletics [*sic*] do to you. It takes over your mind."[28] Not surprisingly, according to a study prepared by two university administrators, "Compared with other students, athletes report having grown less as people at college and having spent limited time at cultural events, pursuing new interests, or meeting new people from different backgrounds."[29]

Defenders of college sports will argue that athletes make a considered choice to trade the long hours of practice for the glory and other rewards that come from playing on a high-profile team. But undergraduates are still adolescents and may not be capable of making sensible and informed decisions about their careers, as Adam Smith pointed out more than 200 years ago in explaining why so many able young men tried to become lawyers despite what were then very dim prospects for success.[30] Many football and basketball players make extraordinarily concentrated efforts to build their bodies and practice for their sport in order to pursue a lucrative career as a professional. A large fraction of those who play for Division IA teams believe they will succeed—vain hope. Less than 2 percent of the football players and only 0.5 percent of the basketball players are ever drafted by a professional team, and fewer still remain a pro long enough to earn an appreciable amount of money.

Several critics have also accused colleges of exploiting their football and basketball players financially. These athletes are the only students on campus whose work brings substantial amounts of revenue to their university. Although they receive an all-expenses-paid scholarship for their efforts, the best players are undoubtedly worth much more to their institutions. Nevertheless, all colleges belonging to the NCAA are bound by a common rule prohibiting them from paying their players more than a full athletic scholarship. Viewed from one perspective, this provision seems like a sensible way to put all competing colleges on an equal footing. From another vantage point, however, the rule amounts to a conspiracy to exploit athletes by preventing them from being compensated at the full value of their services. Several close observers of intercollegiate athletics subscribe to the latter thesis. Even the long-time former president of the NCAA agrees, declaring that "the rewards of success have become so huge that the beneficiaries—the colleges and their staffs—simply will not deny themselves even part of current or future spoils." In fact, he argues, "protecting young people from commercial evils is a transparent excuse for monopoly operations to benefit others."[31]

ATTEMPTED JUSTIFICATIONS

Exploitative or not, big-time athletics have certainly caused many universities to compromise their admissions standards, water down their curricula, and provide many athletes with a pale imitation of a college education if, indeed, they manage to graduate at all. How do university presidents and other academic officials justify such policies, described by *Time Magazine* as "an educational travesty—a farce that devalues every degree and denigrates the mission of higher education"?[32]

The earliest defense (still expressed occasionally) was simply to deny that the problem existed. As Ronald Smith points out in describing the predicament of presidents caught a century ago in the tide of high-visibility college athletics: "The solution to the dilemma, then, was to claim amateurism to the world while in fact accepting professionalism."[33] To this day, the stated mission of the NCAA is "to maintain intercollegiate athletics as an integral part of the educational program and the athlete as an integral part of the student body."[34] Now that the shabby realities of leading football and basketball programs have been publicized over and over again, of course, it is harder to maintain such fictions. Instead, defenders of the status quo have offered a whole series of other reasons to justify existing practices.

One of the oldest justifications has been the alleged capacity of college sports to build the character of student athletes. In the early 1900s, a Harvard faculty committee defended football by declaring that "roughness, unaccompanied by brutality and unfair play, often tends to develop courage, presence of mind, and a manly spirit."[35] Almost a century later, the political columnist, George Will, voiced a similar thought, insisting that "sport is a realm of discipline, skill and excellence and hence has a legitimate role on campuses."[36] In fact, however, there is little proof that big-time athletic programs produce such salutary effects and considerable evidence that high-profile college athletes actually have a far narrower educational experience and report less growth than other students.[37] Most of the research seeking to measure ethical reasoning and moral development has found that athletes do not progress as much as nonathletes.[38] In any case, it is hard to believe that any benefits to character from organized athletics could not be achieved just as well from programs conducted without the intensity and the sacrifice of academic standards that accompany high-pressure college sports. After all, England's battlefield heroes, whose characters were said to be molded on the "playing fields of Eton," never received athletic scholarships to play for public entertainment and institutional profit.

A few coaches, notably John Chaney of Temple University, have offered another defense of intercollegiate athletics, arguing that they provide a way for poor minority youths to obtain a college education. Without doubt, many college teams, especially in football and basketball, are heavily populated by African-Americans. Unfortunately, however, as Mr. Chaney's record at Temple demonstrates, many Division I colleges manage to graduate only a small fraction of their recruited minority athletes. Any university sincerely wishing to educate more minority students would do far better to offer regular scholarships to the best applicants they can find rather than recruit athletes with poor academic credentials and then subject them to the pressures and distractions of high-profile college sports.

Another reason some have given for operating big-time athletic programs is that the publicity and excitement of a winning team can attract more applicants and better students. Those who make this claim rarely pause to explain why a college would want to attract students who chose it because of its football team. Such questions aside, however, the claim itself rests on shaky ground. Several studies in the 1970s and 1980s found that success in basketball and football does not raise the average SAT scores of students at the schools involved.[39] A subsequent study by Andrew Zimbalist, covering the period from 1981–1995, reached the same conclusion.[40] An even later survey in 2001 revealed that athletics are far down the list of things students consider in deciding where to go to college.[41] All in all, therefore, high-visibility sports offer a dubious strategy for improving the quality of the student body, even for schools with the most successful teams.

Still other defenders of college sports point out that winning teams increase school spirit and lift student morale. Again, however, no one has shown that it is necessary to mount a high-pressure program in order to achieve these results. In fact, surveys at selective universities show that athletics are one of the aspects of their college young alumni would most like to see de-emphasized.[42] Far from improving morale, moreover, at least two foundation studies claim that big-time college sports can have destructive effects on undergraduates. As early as 1929, a Carnegie Foundation report concluded that "at no point in the educational process has commercialism in college athletics wrought more mischief than in its effect upon the American undergraduate."[43] The late Ernest Boyer, who served as Commissioner of Education and president of several universities, reached the same conclusion in 1989 in a report on the American college which he wrote as head of the Carnegie Foundation for Teaching: "The cynicism that stems from the abuses in [intercollegiate] athletics infects the rest of student life, from promoting academic dishonesty to the loss of individual ideals."[44]

More than a few college presidents seem to think that a successful athletic program will at least inspire the alumni to give more money to their alma mater. Yet even this hope appears to be groundless. Andrew Zimbalist found that any increases in donations tend to go to the athletic program.[45] A recent study by Sarah Turner, Lauren Meserve, and William Bowen found that there is no statistically significant relation between the won-lost record of the football team and general giving among nonathlete alumni.[46] In fact, in the five private Division IA universities included in the study, improved won-and-lost records resulted in *lower* levels of giving both among former athletes *and* nonathletes.[47] Earlier work on a sample of IA institutions showed that alumni felt that athletics should be de-emphasized and that top alumni donors were just as likely as their classmates to hold that opinion.[48] In short, as Richard Conklin, vice president of Notre Dame, has bluntly observed: "Repeat after me: there is no empirical evidence demonstrating a correlation between athletic department achievement and [alumni] fund raising success."[49]

Despite all the contrary evidence, a number of college presidents cling to the hope that a highly successful football or basketball team will somehow raise the visibility of the university and attract the students, captivate the legislature, and mobilize the donors to lift their institution to a higher rung on the ladder of leading research universities. According to Dan Mote, president of the University of Maryland: "A very visible, very successful athletic program gives you lots of entrees. It changes the understanding of state government, the state legislature, and of the business community and alumni."[50]

In fact, there is no reliable evidence that successful athletic teams raise state appropriations or alumni giving to any appreciable extent. Passing over this point, it would surely require a high degree of athletic success to have any chance of bringing about the hoped-for results. To gain the needed visibility, teams would have to go to a prominent postseason bowl game or advance to the late rounds of the basketball playoffs. Since great universities are not built in a day, such athletic success would have to be repeated over a sustained period. Very few institutions can realistically aspire to such a record; only a few teams, after all, can be ranked as outstanding in a given year, let alone sustain such a rating over a decade or more. Worse yet, history offers few examples of schools that have managed to translate athletic success into a substantially higher position in the academic hierarchy. The universities that have made the most notable progress since 1950—one thinks of Stanford or the campuses other than Berkeley in the California system—did not succeed because of athletics. In fact, there is no university of the first rank that can argue persuasively that its academic success is due in any significant measure to the record of its athletic teams.

All in all, therefore, the chances of using football and basketball to raise a university's academic stature seem highly conjectural at best. What *is* clear is that when universities view their athletic teams not only as a means of making money, but also as the mechanism for improving the status of the entire institution, the pressure to win grows very intense indeed. The single most likely outcome is that academic standards will be a major casualty of the process.

THE PREDICAMENT OF
UNIVERSITY PRESIDENTS

Many university presidents are probably not aware, and do not want to be aware, of the full effect of college sports on their own campus. But most feel at least some discomfort at having to maintain and defend a high-pressure athletic operation, with all the academic compromise it entails. Some would even agree silently with the verdict of a former president of the University of Michigan, who presided over one of the nation's most successful programs: "The mad race for fame and profits through intercollegiate athletics is clearly a fool's quest."[51]

Whatever their true sentiments, sitting presidents feel that they are trapped in a system they are powerless to change. Because they belong to leagues with schedules fixed many years in advance, they cannot reform their current practices without facing humiliation on the playing field, cries of outrage from their boosters, and a sharp drop in the revenues they need to pay for their expensive facilities. Although a majority of their alumni may want to see athletics de-emphasized, a minority do not, and that minority is undoubtedly large and very vocal at a number of institutions. State legislators and substantial segments of the general public also care intensely about college athletics, especially in the South, Midwest, and West. In some regions, football and basketball teams are even important symbols of state pride, and any reform that weakens them competitively could well result in retaliation by the governor and legislature.

University presidents today find it especially hard to stand up against such opposition. All of them are under pressure to raise large sums of money every year from a variety of sources—alumni, state legislatures, federal agencies, and foundations. While multiple funding sources keep a university from becoming too dependent upon a single form of support, they also mean than an institution is in serious trouble if it loses the confidence of any of its key constituencies. Under these circumstances, the typical university president feels peculiarly vulnerable, unwilling to risk offending any significant group or to create the sort of controversy that might lead important donors to think that the administration is somehow "in trouble." Moreover, the mere prospect of having to spend endless hours fighting over athletics is dismaying to campus leaders already fully occupied by the work of keeping their expensive, complicated institutions functioning effectively. It is this combination of limited time and dependence on multiple constituencies that makes so many college presidents today seem reluctant to act boldly or to speak out on controversial issues.* Ironically, most successful presidents in generations past who managed to leave a lasting legacy made their reputation precisely by winning tough, contentious battles over important questions. But those presidents felt much freer to act than their counterparts today, being neither sensitive to so many publics nor burdened by such a multitude of responsibilities.

Under current conditions, then, reforming athletics seems virtually impossible at most Division I schools. At some universities, a serious effort in this direction could cost presidents their jobs. At others, the institution has spent so much money on its sports facilities and infrastructure that it would lose substantial sums by abandoning a high-profile program. At almost all, presidents would have to devote so much time to defending their reforms that they would have to neglect other important responsibilities. In short, they are caught in a situation they may not like but feel unable to change.[52]

---

*Despite repeated criticism from the media for failing to speak publicly on important issues of the day, presidents may have good reason for not declaring themselves on issues of national policy outside the fields of education and research. Critics look back fondly on the giants of yesteryear who participated prominently in national debates but do not always trouble to inquire into the merits of these presidential views. They might be interested to learn that Harvard's greatest president, Charles W. Eliot, argued openly against trade unions, opposed marriage between different ethnic groups, and favored property qualifications for voting. His successor, A. Lawrence Lowell, barred black students from the freshman dormitories and played a prominent role in vigorously opposing the nomination of Louis Brandeis to the Supreme Court. Such examples suggest that university presidents may not provide the best leadership for an educational institution when they take public positions on matters about which they have no special knowledge.

LESSONS FROM THE PLAYING FIELDS

What can intercollegiate sports teach us about the hazards of commercialization? First of all, the saga of big-time athletics reveals that American universities, despite their lofty ideals, are not above sacrificing academic values—even values as basic as admissions standards and the integrity of their courses—in order to make money. Nor will they shrink from exploiting their own students, where necessary, to succeed on the playing field. Although universities regularly proclaim that they seek to help all students develop to their full intellectual potential, they have allowed athletics to consume the lives of their players to such an extent that their athletes cannot possibly obtain anything like the full value of their undergraduate experience. In so doing, universities have compromised the most fundamental purpose of academic institutions.

A few leading private universities manage to attract sufficiently gifted student-athletes to field excellent teams and still maintain high graduation rates, and some schools, especially Catholic colleges, make valiant and successful efforts to help athletes get their degrees. But even the best of these institutions have to make drastic (and growing) compromises with their normal admissions requirements in order to put competitive teams on the field. The rest have to tolerate distressingly low graduation rates and wink at the watered-down courses offered to many of their recruited football and basketball players.

Another lesson that athletics teaches is how illusory the promise of profits can turn out to be. Although revenues from college sports have steadily increased, costs seem to mount at least as rapidly, as the most successful teams set expenditure levels that rival colleges struggle to match. The competition can sometimes reach ludicrous proportions. In 2001, the University of Oregon spent $250,000 for a 100-foot-high billboard near Madison Square Garden in Manhattan, more than 3,000 miles away, in order to promote its quarterback, Joey Harrington, for the Heisman Trophy (given annually to the best college football player in America). Under fire from the faculty for this expenditure, athletic director Bill Moos explained: "As long as the arms race is on, we're going to be in it."[53] Perhaps so, but the "race" must be deeply frustrating to most presidents. So many compromises have been made with academic standards and so many petty scandals have occurred, yet so few institutions have succeeded in making a consistent profit from their athletic programs.

Still another lesson from the saga of athletics is how the lure of money can gradually redefine and legitimate practices that were officially condemned generations before. Early resolutions against charging admission were soon cast aside as the financial possibilities of big-time football became apparent. In 1873, the president of Cornell refused on academic grounds to allow his football team to leave the campus to play another school, adding that "I will not permit thirty men to travel four hundred miles merely to agitate a bag of wind."[54] A century later, universities were allowing their basketball teams to miss classes repeatedly for midweek games in distant locations. Before World War II, Notre Dame refused to accept money for broadcasts of its football games, and turned down an invitation from the Sugar Bowl, arguing that "a post-season game would be played at the expense of many values, physical and academic, which properly belong to the students participating in football."[55] Today, a Notre Dame coach who *fails* to take his team to a postseason bowl is in danger of losing his job, while the institution has a contract with NBC to televise its football games for a sum of more than $6 million per year.[56] From 1906–1948, the NCAA formally condemned the award of athletic scholarships, though violations grew increasingly common. In 1948, it amended the rule to allow athletic awards based on need, only to amend the rule again five years later to permit full scholarships without regard to need.[57] Since then, it has gradually made further concessions to allow additional amounts for "incidentals" and to give coaches greater control over their athletes.

Finally, high-profile athletic programs reveal the limited power of university presidents to reclaim academic values once lucrative commercial practices have won a firm foothold. In 1929, Howard Savage, author of the aforementioned Carnegie Foundation study on college sports, concluded that "the man who is most likely to succeed in uprooting the evils of recruiting and subsidizing is the college president. . . . The university or college that, under capable leadership, makes up its collective mind to cast out these practices, can do so."[58] At the time Savage wrote, this diagnosis may have been correct; Robert Hutchins, after all, managed to abolish football at the University of Chicago and to take his institution out of the Big Ten. Today, however, even as resolute a president as Hutchins would find it impossible to take similar action on a campus committed to big-time football and basketball. This melancholy conclusion underscores the need to think carefully before plunging into some new, seemingly profitable activity. Once such a venture is well under way and the vested interests and financial dependencies start to form, it may already be too late to turn back.

4 | SCIENTIFIC RESEARCH

John Le Carré's latest novel, *The Constant Gardener*, tells of the murder of a young woman in Africa and her husband's valiant efforts to avenge her death. It soon appears that these events all grow out of a major pharmaceutical firm's campaign to develop a new drug for combating tuberculosis.[1] Discovered in a Polish laboratory, the drug looks very promising at first, raising hopes of earning hundreds of millions of dollars. As tests on human subjects begin in Kenya and other African countries, however, problems start to surface. There are side effects. Patients die. One of the scientists who discovered the drug has second thoughts and threatens to go public. Frantic, the company tries to suppress the unfavorable evidence and to buy off, intimidate, or even murder potential critics, such as the young heroine who dies trying to expose the deadly scheme. Meanwhile, the firm contrives to have several well-known academic scientists publish favorable reports about the drug in leading journals without disclosing that the reports were actually written by the company itself and that the purported authors are beneficiaries of lucrative research contracts from the very same source. A remote university in Saskatchewan is persuaded to offer the disaffected discoverer of the drug an amply funded post where she can be watched and induced to keep silent. When she finally speaks out, she is quickly vilified and ostracized by her university and its affiliated hospital, which just happen to have been promised large donations by . . . that's right, the selfsame company.

Le Carré takes care to point out that his book is a work of imagination. He makes no claim that pharmaceutical firms resort to beatings and killings to get new drugs to the market. Still, the author does say that his account "draws on several cases, particularly in the North American continent, where highly qualified medical researchers have dared to disagree with their pharmaceutical paymasters and suffered vilification and persecution for their pains."[2]

This last remark is intriguing. Could such things really happen? If Le Carré's account is not wholly fanciful, how have corporate sponsors actually behaved, and how could universities and their professors get caught up in such compromising ways?

EARLY FEARS

Corporations have become much more involved with university scientists since 1980. Congressional initiatives, such as the Bayh-Dole Act, coupled with the sudden rise of the biogenetics industry, set off a surge of corporate funding for campus-based research and a sudden growth of contacts between professors in the life sciences and interested companies.

Although Congress may have gotten what it wanted, not everyone was pleased with the growing role of industry in supporting academic science. Corporate money, it was said, would subordinate the public aims of research to private ends. Critics warned that universities would impose secrecy and censor research findings to please company sponsors, while exploiting graduate students and corrupting appointments and promotions procedures for commercial gain. In the words of Leslie Glick, founder of Genex Corporation, "Not only will commercial considerations influence decisions about thesis topics and research proposals, but they will likely influence the employment and promotion of professors."[3]

Even more troubling were predictions that corporate money would cause a massive shift of research activity from basic science to applied problems of immediate economic interest. In 1945, Vannevar Bush, in his famous report to President Roosevelt on the future of American science, had pointed out how much the flow of new products and medical treatments depended on a vigorous program of basic research that only universities could provide.[4] Responding to this vision, the federal government came to invest billions of dollars every year in university labs, creating the strongest basic science capability in the world. Suddenly, forty years after the Bush report, critics such as Martin Kenney warned that commercialization was about to destroy the foundations of scientific progress by diverting professors from basic research to more lucrative applied work with high market potential. As he observed at the end of his book, *Biotechnology: The University-Industrial Complex*:

Perhaps the greatest irony will be experienced by U.S. industry itself. As the university is bought and parceled out, basic science in the university will increasingly suffer. The speculative noncommercial scholar will be at a disadvantage, and the intellectual commons so important for producing a trained labor force and the birthplace of new ideas will be eroded and polluted. Industry will then discover that by being congenitally unable to control itself and having no restraints placed upon it by the public sector, it has polluted its own reservoir.[5]

To what extent have these dire prophecies come to pass? Certainly not to anything like the degree that critics such as Kenney and Glick predicted. There is little evidence that professors have steered a significant number of their graduate students into commercial research to promote their own financial interests. Nor have there been many documented reports of universities compromising their appointments and promotions standards to retain professors doing work of great commercial potential. Skeptics would even be hard put to show that research priorities have shifted in any substantial way to favor applied research at the expense of more fundamental inquiry.[6] The percentage of university R&D devoted to basic research has remained fairly constant since the late 1970s. While corporate support has grown, it still makes up less than 10 percent of all university research and hence does not significantly affect the overall balance of priorities. If certain valuable fields of basic inquiry receive less money than they should, such results are likely to reflect the shortsightedness of government authorities (or perhaps foundation officials) rather than the malign influence of business.

Individual scientists have also resisted rushing pell-mell into the arms of corporate sponsors. The share of all life-science faculty receiving at least some research funding from industry has stayed close to 25 percent since 1985 (and less than half of those who do receive such funding obtain more than one-quarter of their total support from business).[7] Comprehensive faculty surveys suggest that the percentage of life-science professors serving as scientific advisors to companies has not gone up appreciably.[8] Only 7 percent of the faculty members in a 1985 survey reported owning equity in private companies, and later fragmentary data do not indicate that the number is increasing.[9] It is true that faculty members with industry support are more likely than other scientists to be influenced by commercial considerations in choosing their research topics (35 percent v. 14 percent).[10] On the other hand, such researchers publish more than their colleagues in peer-reviewed journals and spend just as much time teaching students.[11] Overall, these findings bear out the conclusion of one team of investigators that canvassed life-sciences professors in leading universities: "there is little evidence in our survey to suggest that most life scientists are more interested in commercial activities than in traditional scientific endeavors . . . or that a new kind of entrepreneurial scholar has taken over in universities."[12]

If any tie with business proved to be a problem for research universities, one would have thought that it would be corporate consulting by the faculty. The prevailing rules on most campuses actually seem to invite faculty members to consult, since professors continue to receive their regular salaries during days spent far from the university earning extra money advising companies. The standard rule for outside activity—only one day per week—is open to several possible interpretations and is hard to enforce in any event, since faculty members will stoutly resist punching time clocks or handing in weekly timesheets.

Every campus has professors who do flout the rules and constantly spend much time away from their offices. Since cases of this kind attract attention, they can easily give the impression that most professors endlessly gallivant about making money at the expense of their teaching and re-search. Studies of the actual amount of paid consulting, however, fail to confirm this impression. Very few faculty members regularly consult more than the permissible one day per week, and the average compensation received by consultants in almost every field is less then one-tenth of their average academic salary.[13] Those who advise corporations teach as much, take on as many committee assignments, and publish more than colleagues who do not consult.[14] Contrary to what one might expect, one recent study found that life-science faculty members in highly ranked departments who consult with industry are *less* likely than their colleagues to be influenced by commercial considerations in choosing their research agenda.[15]

Apparently, then, the values that have traditionally inspired academic scientists have generally been strong enough to withstand the desire to grow rich. University researchers are not averse to making money on the side through consulting, and some may even decide at one point or another to work for a company where opportunities to do good science seem particularly promising. But if they have to choose between the kind of research they enjoy and earning large sums of money, they rarely prefer the latter. For almost all academic scientists, the respect of colleagues and the satisfactions that come from making important advances in knowledge continue to count above all else. In addition, it must be said, government funding agencies (and many corporate executives, too) understand the importance of basic science and have no desire to damage its vitality as the essential seedbed of future commercial applications.

Far from worrying that university scientists will be corrupted by business, some observers believe that active collaboration with colleagues in industry is actually useful in stimulating basic research. As Henry Etzkowitz has put it: "What is new in the present situation is that many academic scientists no longer believe in the necessity of an isolated 'ivory tower' to the working out of the logic of scientific discovery."[16] This sentiment is more than a rationalization on the part of university researchers eager to collect their consulting fees. It reflects a genuine sense that the process of scientific exploration has become a much more collaborative process, requiring input and stimulation from a wide variety of sources, of which some, at least, may reside in the more practical world of industrial science.[17] Today, talented scientists who are worthy collaborators are more likely than in the past to work for a company, at least for part of their professional careers. In certain fields of work, such as the development of new drugs, collaboration with industry is actually essential, since companies often have databases, vast libraries of relevant compounds, sophisticated computer models, and other research materials that university laboratories do not have and that scientists must be able to use to do their work.

As collaboration increases, giving rise to spectacular commercial successes such as Silicon Valley, the Research Triangle, or the Austin Miracle, voices can be heard urging more aggressive efforts to increase and improve technology transfer. Aiding business in this way is increasingly recognized as an explicit part of the mission of research universities. Some advocates would have campus officials acknowledge this responsibility even more strongly by counting contributions to technology transfer—obtaining patents, starting companies, serving on scientific advisory boards— as a positive factor in appointments and promotions decisions. Others are not so sure. They worry about diverting talented scientists from basic research and other problems that could result from becoming too closely involved in commercial activities. This difference in outlook is far from resolved.

SECRECY

Although the worst fears of critics have not materialized, the rise of corporate funding has not been trouble-free. One of the most serious problems is increased secrecy. Firms that offer research support naturally want to keep any commercially valuable results from falling into a competitor's hands. Accordingly, company officials regularly insist that information concerning the work they support be kept in confidence while the research is going on and for a long enough time thereafter to allow them to decide whether to file for a patent. In addition, they may consider other bits of valuable information unsuitable for patenting and treat them as permanent trade secrets instead. For example, firms often share unpatented materials or techniques with academic colleagues only on condition that they be kept confidential indefinitely.

Although the results of university research may eventually be made public, companies continually press for more and more restrictions while the research they support is under way in an effort to keep any word of new discoveries from leaking prematurely to their competitors. Many firms try to prohibit the researchers they fund from speaking about their work at conferences. Some corporate agreements can be interpreted to require scientists to obtain clearance before merely talking on the telephone with colleagues. A few professors have actually declared their laboratories off-limits to colleagues and students in their own departments. While no one can measure the impact of such restrictions with precision, the likely effect is to inhibit scientific progress, at least to some extent, by limiting the flow of information and ideas that investigators need in order to advance their work.[18]

Surprisingly, many universities, their affiliated hospitals, and other biomedical research organizations have not done much to keep secrecy to the minimum necessary to protect legitimate commercial interests. In one comprehensive study, only 12 percent of these institutions had policies specifying clear time limits on keeping discoveries secret.[19] Some had no written policy at all. Others do not rigorously enforce their own rules. As a result, company research directors report that they seldom have difficulty obtaining as much secrecy as they want.

Survey results confirm that corporate funding has led to more secrecy than the strict necessities of business require. Although most observers believe that one or two months after completion of the research will give companies enough time to decide whether to seek a patent, 58 percent of corporate sponsors in one large study admitted to insisting regularly on delays of more than six months.[20] Nearly one in five life-science professors admitted that they had delayed publication by more than six months for commercial reasons.[21] Of course, scientists may refuse to talk about their work in order to preserve their lead over rival investigators or for other reasons having nothing to do with commercial gain. Nevertheless, the proportion delaying publication for more than six months was substantially greater (27 percent v. 17 percent) among researchers with industry funding, and the same pattern prevailed among faculty who refused to share research results and kept trade secrets.[22] A small but significant number of faculty members in the survey (12.5 percent) reported that they had themselves been denied access to research results or products by university researchers during the past three years.[23]

Scientists are also concerned over the time required to obtain permission to share cell lines and other research materials. The delays involved sometimes cause investigators to give up in disgust, especially when they need to borrow from several sources to proceed with their research. Companies, too, are up in arms. According to a report from a working group to the Director of the National Institutes of Health, "virtually every firm that we spoke with believed that restricted access to research tools is impeding the rapid advance of research and that the problem is getting worse."[24] Ironically, universities were accused of being among the worst offenders. "Over and over again, firms complained to us that universities 'wear the mortarboard' when they seek access to [research] tools developed by others, yet they impose the same sorts of restrictions when they enter into agreements to give firms access to their own tools."[25]

Apparently, universities often hold up requests for materials in an effort to obtain a slice of any revenue that grows out of the companies' research. When they share with universities, companies, for their part, insist on safeguards to keep their materials out of the hands of researchers under contract to rival firms. The net result is a far cry from the ideal community of scholars, freely sharing their ideas and materials in a common quest for greater knowledge and understanding.

CONFLICTS OF INTEREST

Conflicts of interest in science arise in "situations in which financial or other personal considerations may compromise, or have the appearance of compromising, an investigator's professional judgment in conducting or reporting research."[26] Such conflicts can easily result from the growing ties between corporations and university researchers. Faculty members, especially in the life sciences, may own a significant share of stock in a company for which they do research (perhaps a firm they founded to commercialize one of their own discoveries). Short of ownership, professors may test the products of a firm from which they have received significant amounts of research funding or obtained a lucrative consulting agreement. All these relationships provide reasons to favor the company involved and hence create conflicts that threaten the objectivity of scientists when they advise the government or publish research results on matters of financial significance to their corporate sponsor. Even if the scientists involved are completely honest and unbiased, their financial interests may give the *appearance* of bias and hence undermine the credibility of their work.

Conflicts of interest have attracted particular attention in research to test new drugs or medical procedures where human subjects are involved. Testing of this kind has become a major enterprise involving some 60,000 trials and 14 million human subjects per year at a total annual cost of several billion dollars. Such a large undertaking involving such high financial stakes is bound to give rise to instances of questionable behavior. In one highly publicized case, a research fellow in a Harvard-affiliated hospital, Scheffer Tseng, turned out to have minimized unfavorable results in a clinical study to test a dry-eye medication. It then came to light that both Tseng and his supervisor owned stock in the company that produced the medication, stock Tseng sold after his published test results had driven up the price but before the negative findings were revealed.

Conflicts of interest can turn up in more tragic circumstances. In 1999, Jesse Gelsinger, an eighteen-year-old patient in a gene therapy trial at the University of Pennsylvania Medical School, died in the course of the experiment. As it happened, the director of the institute conducting the research was the founder and a major stockholder in the company that funded the research. The university, too, was a stockholder, having been given an equity share by the company. Although the director did not participate personally in the trials, both he and the university stood to gain financially if the therapy being tested proved to be successful.

In most types of scientific research, any bias in the work performed is likely to be discovered sooner or later when other investigators replicate the studies. In clinical research, however, scientists with financial interests in the results may be too anxious to enroll patients in hazardous experiments involving the products or companies with which they have ties. In this event, human subjects may be put at risk before anyone is even aware of the conflicts involved.

Scientists with corporate ties naturally deny that financial interests will have any effect on their scientific work. Nevertheless, a number of investigators have shown that researchers reporting on the efficacy of drugs produced by companies in which they have an interest are more likely to report favorable results than scientists without such ties.[27] Other studies have shown that clinical trials funded by drug companies are far less likely than independently funded trials to arrive at unfavorable conclusions.[28]

In 1989, the National Institutes of Health proposed strict new rules to minimize financial conflicts of interest in research funded by the government. The proposals quickly came under heavy fire from university scientists. Eventually, the NIH retreated and produced a much weaker set of guidelines that merely required investigators to disclose financial conflicts to their universities but allowed the latter to decide what further restrictions to impose.

Opponents have made several arguments against stricter conflict-of-interest rules.[29] Some maintain that it is unfair to assume that scientists will be guilty of bias just because they have a financial interest. Others point out that there is no reason to single out financial conflicts for regulation, since scientists have always had to contend with temptations, such as the desire for fame or promotion, that can lead them to overstate or distort their findings. Still others insist that the best cure for biased results is the time-honored process in science of testing and replicating published research findings.

None of these arguments is persuasive, especially for research involving human subjects. Everyone agrees that it is wise to prohibit judges and government officials from making decisions on questions in which they have financial interests, even though many of these public servants could doubtless keep their investments from affecting their judgment. Since no one can tell whose judgment will be affected and whose will not, the standard practice is to remove all doubt by preventing conflicting interests from arising in the first place. By the same token, there is no unfairness in holding scientists to similar rules to reduce the risk of financial influence.

The other arguments against limiting conflicts are no more persuasive. The fact that all scientists face a human temptation to win fame by exaggerating their results is hardly a reason not to counter potential biases that *can* be easily removed or disclosed in advance. Although some inaccuracies and misrepresentations will eventually be detected by other investigators, not all of them will be found.

Even if they are, discovering errors by investigators with undisclosed financial conflicts will still damage the credibility of university science. Worse yet, setting the record straight at some later date will do nothing for innocent patients whose health may have been put at risk by investigators using them as subjects to test some potentially lucrative new treatment.

Most people now agree that rules are needed to guard against conflicts of interest. But controversy continues over exactly what the rules should contain. Some argue that it is enough to require clear disclosure both to scientific journals and to human subjects before enrolling them in an experiment. Others strenuously disagree, insisting that the only way to eliminate the harmful effects of bias is to prohibit financial conflicts altogether.

Whatever the answer, academic institutions do not seem to be doing nearly enough to protect against the risks involved. According to one study published in 2000, only 3 of 250 medical schools and research institutions insisted that investigators disclose their financial conflicts to patients before enrolling them in clinical experiments or drug trials.[30] Only 7 percent of these institutions required their researchers to disclose such conflicts to journals publishing their research.[31] Only one of the ten leading medical schools receiving the greatest amounts of federal funding flatly prohibited investigators from doing clinical research on products of firms with which they had significant financial ties.[32] Most of these merely required disclosure to university officials.

In addressing these issues, universities do not come to the task with entirely clean hands, for they, too, may have financial interests that could conceivably bias the results. For example, Columbia, Duke, and several other medical schools have formed consortia to bid for contracts from pharmaceutical firms to test new drugs. In many cases, the principal purpose is not to secure opportunities for cutting-edge research, but rather to earn money that can be used for other purposes. Schools that benefit in this way clearly have a financial stake in retaining the business of the companies whose products they test. To that extent, they have an incentive to avoid results that will disappoint their corporate sponsors. Nevertheless, like individual investigators, medical schools seem unwilling to admit that their financial interests could possibly affect the results of research performed within their walls.

CORPORATE EFFORTS TO INFLUENCE RESEARCH RESULTS

Efforts to test the effects of new drugs create additional risks not commonly found in university research. Clinical tests can enhance the value of a potentially lucrative product or destroy it. As a result, the sponsoring firm will often have a huge financial stake in the outcome of the research. Of course, companies will hardly want to market a drug that is actually dangerous to health. But no such inhibition exists in the case of trials to determine whether a brand-name drug is superior to generic substitutes or whether a medical device or procedure is truly efficacious or harmlessly ineffective. Even in the case of potentially dangerous products, corporate officials can be so blinded by the prospect of financial gain that they use poor judgment in working with academic researchers conducting tests.

Whatever the reason, drug companies sometimes employ highly questionable methods in an effort to gain the credibility of an academically run clinical trial while retaining control over the results.[33] Some firms insist on keeping all the data or helping to design the test. Some actually ghostwrite drafts of the final report for academic researchers to review prior to publication, a dangerous practice in view of the many subtle ways in which a study can be written up to place the company's product in a more favorable light. Other companies try to insert provisions in the research contract giving them the right to approve all material prior to publishing the results. None of these practices seems consistent with the standards universities need to protect the objectivity and accuracy of their research.

Even more troubling are a handful of cases involving heavy-handed attempts by drug companies to suppress unfavorable findings by university scientists. For example, Betty Dong of the University of California, San Francisco, received a grant from a pharmaceutical firm to determine whether its expensive drug Synthroid was in fact superior to cheaper generic alternatives. Against expectations, including her own, she found no significant difference (which meant that patients were paying several hundred million dollars more per year for Synthroid than they needed to spend). Informed of these embarrassing results, the company accused Dong of numerous methodological errors and unspecified ethical lapses and even hired a private investigator to look for conflicts of interest (which proved to be nonexistent). When Dong went ahead and submitted her findings to a professional journal, the company threatened suit, invoking a clause in the research agreement she had signed prohibiting publication without the firm's consent. Although the university had never reviewed the contract or warned her not to sign, it declined to assist her, leaving her to fight the company alone. Only after seven years did she finally succeed in publishing her paper.

Another professor, Nancy Olivieri, of the University of Toronto, met a similar fate, experiencing harassment much akin to the trials of the woman scientist in Le Carré's *The Constant Gardener*. In her capacity as university professor and researcher at the University's Hospital for Sick Children, Olivieri signed a contract with Canada's largest pharmaceutical firm, Apotex, to perform clinical trials on a drug to treat thalassemia patients. The contract contained a clause prohibiting her from publicizing results for a stipulated period without the company's permission. Despite the agreement, she insisted on making her findings known (with the approval of the hospital's Research Ethics Board) when they seemed to indicate that the drug she was testing was not only less effective than originally thought, but even potentially hazardous to patients.

As in the case of Betty Dong, the drug company accused Olivieri of deviating from the research protocol and tried to discourage her from reporting her findings by threatening legal action and canceling her research contract. In addition, a faculty associate sought to discredit her by sending disparaging anonymous letters to colleagues and the media and by publishing contrary findings without either informing her or disclosing that his work was being generously funded by Apotex. For her pains, she was falsely accused by her hospital of failing to observe hospital regulations, suspended from her position as program director, and directed, along with her supporters on the staff, not to discuss her problems publicly.

Throughout these controversies, the University of Toronto remained largely uninvolved, despite a flood of unfavorable publicity about the treatment of Olivieri by its affiliated teaching hospital. It then appeared that the university and Apotex had for some years been in discussions about a multimillion-dollar gift to the university and its teaching hospitals. Only after another firestorm of publicity and the intervention of distinguished scientists from Britain and the United States did the university finally intervene and mediate an agreement to have the hospital restore Olivieri's authority over patient care and research and acknowledge her academic freedom.

Olivieri and Dong are by no means the only investigators who have been pressured by companies; there are plenty of anecdotes involving researchers threatened by lawsuits or attacks on their reputation in an effort to suppress unfavorable results. No one knows how extensive this problem is, since no one can be sure how many scientists have quietly succumbed to pressure and suppressed their findings rather than undergo the harassment and delay endured by Dong and Olivieri.[34] Still, the problems of undue influence and manipulation of research are great enough to have persuaded ten leading medical journals to take action. In 2001, they agreed not to accept any articles reporting the results of clinical trials unless the sponsoring company and the authors give satisfactory assurances that the sponsor has not tried to suppress unfavorable findings or otherwise influence the results.[35] Explaining the policy, the editor of the *Journal of the American Medical Association* declared: "I am not against pharmaceutical companies. What I object to is the use of my journal as an advertisement mechanism rather than a vehicle for the distribution of sound medical science."[36]

The Dong and Olivieri cases also raise questions about how willing medical schools and their affiliated hospitals are to resist pressure from corporate donors and how careful they are to protect their faculty from signing agreements with undue restrictions on publication. Faculty members rarely read the fine print of their research contracts, written as they are in the dense prose to which the legal profession is so famously attached. One contract officer for a group of major research hospitals estimates that 30–50 percent of all proposed agreements submitted by companies contain inappropriately broad secrecy clauses.[37] Without proper university oversight, many of these provisions are bound to find their way into the final contract.

Drug testing for pharmaceutical firms is not the only example of high-stakes research. Nutritionists investigating the health effects of particular foods can dampen the prospects of entire industries, just as epidemiologists changed the lives of tobacco manufacturers by demonstrating the link between cigarettes and cancer. Environmental scientists evaluating the effects of emissions can publish findings that bring about extremely costly regulations for manufacturers. Investigators studying the existence of global warming can drastically alter the future of the energy industry.

Unlike drug testing, however, most of the research just described is funded primarily by the government, not by industry. As a result, commercial interests do not have as much leverage over the results. But some companies try to influence the public debate by offering research funding to scientists who have views—or show promise of having views—that are favorable to the industry involved. Thus, investigators are often aware that if their work on controversial subjects turns out to be sympathetic to important corporate interests, money for their future work will be assured.

This state of affairs carries obvious risks for academic science. The clearest danger is that investigators who receive corporate funding for their research may be influenced in ways that favor the industry. They may not alter their findings deliberately to retain the favor of company sponsors. Having received such support, however, they may be subtly affected when they decide how strongly to word a conclusion, how much to emphasize possible qualifications and contrary interpretations, or whether to mention potential (but unproven) new risks. At the very least, industry funding can magnify the voice of those who receive it and encourage them to continue their research and be more outspoken and more vigorous in expounding their views.

Such tactics can confuse the public and distort the debate about important issues. For example, one survey investigating the wide divergence of views on the health effects of passive smoke found that 74 percent of the studies finding no adverse effects were written by authors with ties to the tobacco industry. Of the authors with tobacco ties, 94 percent found that passive smoke was not harmful to health, while only 13 percent of those without tobacco ties reached the same conclusion.[38]

Corporate efforts to influence public debate do more than muddy the waters. As the funding sources for the research become known, along with other links between the authors and interested companies, people become more skeptical of what they read from supposedly disinterested scholars. Eventually, confidence in all academic research may suffer, especially if the investigators who join the debate and testify before Congress fail to reveal the identity of their sponsors.

LESSONS LEARNED AND NOT YET LEARNED

Looking back, the record of commercializing academic research over the past twenty years is instructive in several ways. Now that efforts by universities to patent scientific discoveries have become well established, the financial results are reminiscent of intercollegiate athletics. Most universities have not earned much money from royalties; the odds of making anything substantial from patenting a new discovery are extremely small. Still, the extraordinary success of a few patents and the many millions of dollars in royalties earned each year by a small minority of schools are enough to keep scores of institutions scouring their labs for commercially valuable innovations. In this respect, commercial incentives have succeeded in encouraging universities to do a much better job of serving the public interest.

At the same time, using the promise of financial gain to bring about socially useful results is a risky enterprise. While Le Carré may have engaged in flights of fiction by having pharmaceutical companies resort to murder and beatings, most of the other transgressions he described have their counterparts in real life. Universities have paid a price for industry support through excessive secrecy, periodic exposés of financial conflict, and corporate efforts to manipulate or suppress research results. No consensus has yet emerged on how to contain these threats to academic science. Differences of opinion persist over how best to deal with conflicts of interest arising from the financial ties of investigators or of the university itself. Rules relating to secrecy are often lax, weakly enforced, and seldom applied to restrictions companies attach to research done through consulting agreements or corporate gifts. In the face of pressure from corporate sponsors to influence the results of high-stakes clinical research, institutional safeguards have proved inadequate in a disturbing number of cases.

Most universities have not done all they should to protect the integrity of their research. Many have not even shown that they are seriously concerned about doing so. As in athletics, officials have been willing to cut corners and wink at potential problems in an effort to gain additional resources. Unlike athletics, however, commercialization of research is still relatively new, and universities are not yet bound irrevocably to indefensible policies. Only time will tell whether they manage to do a better job of maintaining appropriate standards for science than they have done in upholding academic values on their playing fields.

5 | EDUCATION

In 1998, Meyer Feldberg, dean of the Columbia Business School, received a phone call from an old friend, Michael Milken, impresario of junk bonds, master of the leveraged buy-out, and active again after twenty-two months in a federal prison for securities law violations.[1] Milken was calling to urge Feldberg to talk with another mutual friend, Andrew Rosenfield, lawyer, University of Chicago trustee, and currently operating as founder and CEO of an online company interested in distance education. What Milken and Rosenfield wanted was a collaboration that would allow Columbia professors to offer on-line courses in exchange for royalties from fees collected from subscribing students. Signing up Columbia would give the new venture instant credibility and make it easier to enlist other leading universities with the kind of "brand names" that could attract large enrollments of students here and abroad.

Feldberg was intrigued. For him, on-line education meant opportunities to expand the range of his faculty. "I want to reach a global audience," he said. So long as his faculty could only teach within the limited space available on Columbia's New York City campus, "our opportunities to extend our reach to the student and corporate market-place [will be] constrained by our physical capacity." Besides, added Rosenfield, "universities don't have multi-media expertise. For them to spend tens to hundreds of millions of dollars to experiment in a new field would not be prudent. We are prepared to spend tens to hundreds of millions of dollars."

Several months later, Columbia and the on-line company—now called U.Next—signed a contract. According to its terms, Columbia professors would teach on-line and U.Next could identify them using the Columbia name. Columbia would receive royalties based on the size of the audience with a minimum guarantee of $20 million payable after five years. Feldberg, eager to share in what he thought might become a financial bonanza, insisted on a right to convert all royalties into U.Next stock.

Negotiated behind closed doors without consultation with faculty or students, the contract drew a mixed response when it finally became public knowledge. An editorial in the Columbia Business School student paper praised it as a bold, forward-looking venture. A dissenting view, published anonymously, referred to Feldberg as a "spreadsheet jockey" and questioned whether he was harming Columbia's stature at the expense of students and faculty. Controversial or not, the agreement had its intended effect on other leading universities. Fortified by Columbia's example, such institutions as the University of Chicago, Carnegie Mellon, and the London School of Economics quickly signed on with U.Next under terms similar to those agreed to by Feldberg.

The U.Next experience could lead one to believe that higher education is about to enter a new and vastly lucrative era. It is still too early, however, to speak definitively about the benefits and costs that new technology will bring to enterprising universities. But useful clues may be gleaned from the record of earlier attempts to make a profit from educational programs.

A BRIEF HISTORY OF EDUCATION FOR PROFIT

However novel the U.Next venture may be, there is nothing new about universities trying to earn some extra money from their teaching. Although American universities have traditionally operated on a not-for-profit basis, many of them began long ago to develop educational programs that would yield a surplus they could use for other purposes. As early as 1892, William Rainey Harper, President of the University of Chicago, created a correspondence school for individuals who could not afford to leave their homes and jobs to learn on campus. Other universities followed suit. In an effort to attract more students, institutions such as Columbia and the University of Chicago advertised widely and hired traveling salesmen, who, according to Abraham Flexner, were not above resorting to a "hard sell" to gain and retain customers.[2] When students dropped out of the courses after a few lessons, as many did, the university allowed no refund although it incurred no further cost. In this way, institutions could earn a profit they could use for other programs.

Observers disagreed about the quality of correspondence education. Some long-time veterans of the correspondence movement argued that most instructors were recruited from the university's regular faculty and that students performed as well when learning by mail as they did when attending classes on campus.[3] Critics such as Flexner strongly disagreed, claiming that the quality of instruction was well below the normal level on campus and that the marketing methods used by some institutions were beneath the dignity of a true university.* Eventually, the critics prevailed, and university-sponsored correspondence programs went into decline.

The differences of opinion over the quality of correspondence instruction were never finally resolved. But even its defenders admitted that teachers were often slow in grading papers and responding to student questions.[4] And no one denies that most universities paid their teaching staff on a piece-rate basis (at low rates) so that they could keep all the tuitions but save any further costs of students who dropped out before completing the course.

In addition to launching correspondence courses, President Harper was also a pioneer in the development of campus-based extension programs for working students who could only attend classes during evenings or weekends. Many universities followed Harper's example and started programs of their own, most of which have survived and flourish to this day. Extension divisions are usually operated on a for-profit basis, especially in private universities where some programs manage to earn millions of dollars each year for their parent institutions. State universities have been less inclined to treat their extension divisions as a profit center, but this tendency may be changing as public higher education feels increasingly pinched for money.[5]

Without a doubt, extension schools have served many

---

*Flexner was unsparing in his criticism. In his words, "Columbia, which should be a bulwark against uniformity and the home of intellectual integrity, independence, and idiosyncrasy, plays the purely commercial game of the merchant whose sole concern is profit. . . . That the prestige of the University of Chicago should be used to bamboozle well-meaning but untrained persons with the notion that they can receive a high school or a college education [by mail] is scandalous" (*Universities: American, English, German* [1930], pp. 133–34, 147).

students well, enabling some to earn degrees without having to leave their job and others to gain a new vocational skill, learn a foreign language, or simply pursue a special interest in literature, history, or filmmaking. Within their own institutions, however, extension programs are rarely treated the same as other faculties. On most campuses, the administration regards them as marginal.[6] Their courses are generally created to meet a public demand and are discontinued if they cannot attract more than a few students. At private universities, in particular, officials often judge their extension school deans primarily by the size of the surplus they give to the central administration and regularly push them to increase their contributions. Even universities that do not try to make a profit pay their extension instructors only modestly at best and rarely offer any financial aid to students.

At the graduate level, professional schools have programs of their own for established practitioners. Some of them are brief refresher courses, such as those for lawyers and doctors, that keep participants abreast of new developments in their field. Some last slightly longer and teach their students to master a new technique or skill. The most ambitious are "transformational," such as the multiweek programs to help rising business executives make the transition from specialists in marketing, production, or finance to general managers exercising broad authority over company operations.

Programs for professionals and others in midcareer have become very popular during the last few decades. At Harvard, for example, some 18,000 students are enrolled in regular degree programs, but over 60,000 more come to the campus for a few days, a few weeks, or an entire year. Most of them are older men and women already established in their careers. These students can be quite unusual: thirty members of the Russian Duma, for example, wishing to learn something about how to serve effectively in a democratic legislature; reporters from around the world enjoying a sabbatical to reflect on their calling and gain new background knowledge for future assignments; military officers taking courses to prepare themselves for their next tour of duty in the Pentagon or in an overseas command.

Many of these courses earn a handsome surplus for the sponsoring faculties. Executive programs for corporate officials are the most lucrative of all. They have also become highly competitive, as business schools vie not only with each other, but also with consulting firms or with the "corporate universities" that many large companies operate with impressive campuses of their own.[7] Despite the competition, leading management schools with well-known brand names can earn many millions of dollars per year from their executive programs. The best schools can pick and choose to the point of offering only programs that are intellectually challenging to their professors. Schools of lesser reputation are rarely so fortunate. Often, they earn only a modest surplus and may have to cajole their faculty into giving repetitive courses of an elementary kind to entry-level trainees.

Recently, a new and promising market has emerged involving "customized" courses to serve the special needs of particular corporations.[8] Such offerings range from basic classes for lower-level executives in subjects such as marketing or finance to special sessions to help the highest officers of a company think creatively about some new challenge facing their organization. The resulting programs depart from traditional practice by allowing the company to choose the students who participate and to work closely with faculty instructors designing course materials that reflect the special problems and conditions of the client firm.

Although such close corporate involvement in developing an educational program is unusual, it is not particularly worrisome. The interests of the company and the educational standards of the university almost always coincide. Clearly, the company will want the highest quality of instruction for its own executives. Its motive in helping to design the curriculum is not to manipulate the audience but to make sure that the program addresses accurately and effectively the problems most relevant to the firm. Such collaboration can not only improve the quality of the program, but also give faculty members exceptional opportunities to learn about emerging problems relevant to their professional interests.

A different situation has arisen in the field of medicine. Medical schools have long conducted continuing education programs that keep practicing physicians abreast of new developments in diagnosis and cure. Most states require doctors to complete a prescribed amount of such advanced training in order to keep their license to practice. In helping to meet this demand, many medical schools operate their continuing education courses at a profit to subsidize other activities.

Anxious to keep down costs but still provide attractive programs, medical faculties are quick to respond to offers of help from willing corporations. They need not look far. Hoping to win the favor of doctors who regularly prescribe drugs and other treatments, pharmaceutical firms and medical supply companies are only too willing to participate in these programs by paying part of the cost, supplying equipment, and setting up tables to display their wares.[9] Often, corporate sponsors provide lists of speakers who are paid for by the company and supplied with written materials and slides prepared by company personnel. With the willing connivance of the school, sponsoring firms frequently treat the doctors attending the sessions to lavish meals, evening entertainment, golf privileges, and even ocean cruises. By now, a full third of the total cost of continuing medical education is paid for by interested corporations.

One can hardly avoid asking whether such heavy corporate involvement will not corrupt the educational process by turning the entire program into a massive promotional exercise for the sponsors' products. Both medical schools and participating companies vigorously deny such a charge. They point out that the speakers subsidized by the sponsoring firms are almost always established academic experts, that accrediting agencies forbid any corporate influence over program content, and that the doctors in attendance will quickly detect any effort to favor particular products and protest loudly. These responses are reassuring. Still, the involvement of sponsoring companies is so extensive and the commercial interests of the sponsors are so obvious that serious doubts remain. After all, why would corporations contribute hundreds of millions of dollars to the education of physicians if they did not expect to reap a handsome reward?

THE INTERNET

The most dramatic new development in the field of nontraditional education is the growth of distance learning using the Internet.[10] With the Internet, lectures can be transmitted anywhere in the world, while giving students a chance to ask questions and get rapid answers by e-mail. Often, not only can students watch lectures, they can also engage in seminar discussions through teleconferencing with other participants residing in widely scattered locations.

By the year 2000, education via the Internet was already a $2 billion business, growing by 40 percent per year. According to one observer, "The Internet is revolutionizing the way Americans learn. Driven by an information economy, where knowledge is the hot commodity, the online education market is booming. Working professionals can log on at any hour, bone up on finance, accounting or engineering skills, and study with professors from elite institutions."[11] Larry Ellison, CEO of Oracle, looks forward to a future in which e-learning will overcome the "wild inefficiencies of American higher education" by offering "million dollar salaries for a few star professors and access to the best teaching for millions and millions of students all over the world."[12] According to Peter Drucker, "Already we are beginning to deliver more lectures and classes off campus via satellite or two-way video at a fraction of the cost. The college won't survive as a residential institution. Today's buildings are hopelessly unsuited and totally unneeded."[13]

Sweeping predictions of this kind are not new; they have regularly accompanied the birth of new technologies throughout the twentieth century. In the 1920s, Thomas Edison argued that motion pictures would replace ordinary campus lectures.[14] Fifteen years later, representatives of the University of Iowa declared that "it is no imaginary dream to picture the school of tomorrow as an entirely different institution from that of today because of the use of radio in teaching."[15] In the1950s, John Davies, chair of the National University Extension Association, remarked that "never has the opportunity of reaching into the actual home been so startling as the opportunity given through television."[16]

All of these statements turned out to be wildly exaggerated. Of all the new technologies, only the humble audio-tape won a substantial following in the United States for educational purposes. Still, the Internet does have features that make it unusually attractive as a teaching vehicle. Compared with radio, television, and other technologies, it allows instructors to update material more easily and tailor teaching programs to suit the needs of particular audiences. Above all, the medium is interactive, permitting students to communicate with each other and with instructors either at a single designated time or whenever they choose. In some respects, the Internet may actually be superior to a regular seminar because it can elicit more considered responses and wider participation, especially by students reluctant to express themselves in a classroom before their peers.[17] In certain classes, such as those involving complex lab experiments, the new technology can allow students to familiarize themselves with equipment in advance or observe and manipulate simulated material in ways more effective than normal teaching methods allow. In courses assigning problems with exact answers, students can receive instant feedback for homework submitted on-line.

Definitive studies of Internet education are not yet available, but most existing assessments suggest that students can learn as much using this medium as they can in a regular on-campus class.[18] It may not yet be possible to equal a truly well-taught Socratic discussion in a leading law school or the active give and take of a successful college seminar. Still, such on-campus experiences are not typical of the length and breadth of American higher education. In describing their college experiences, many undergraduates would probably echo the sentiments of this senior from a large state university.

In my four years at . . . , I have had exactly four classes
with under twenty-five students and a real professor in
charge. All the rest of my courses have been jumbo lectures with hundreds of students and a professor miles
away, or classes with TAs [graduate student teaching assis-
tants], or not regular faculty, people who come in off the
street and teach a course or two. Very few of the TAs or
these part-times know squat about how to teach, some of
them don't even know anything about their subjects.[19]

It is quite likely that modern technology can provide learning opportunities that are more than a match for those just
described by this disgruntled undergraduate.

Yet for all its attractive features, the Internet is not in
every respect an effective substitute for traditional university
education. Much that is valuable in a student's development still comes from experiences that are hard to equal
electronically: chance encounters over dinner; intense
collaborative experiences obtained through extracurricular
activities; unstructured discussions in seminars; or close
personal relations with friends and fellow students.[20] The
Internet may do well at performing some educational functions, but it is not yet clear how effective it will be at foster-
ing interest in new ideas, or building a commitment to
helping others, or developing leadership talents. Nor is it
clear how successful the new technology will be at keeping
students enrolled. The subtle communal pressure of taking
courses on a campus in the company of classmates gives
students a reason to persevere and not abandon their studies
when temptations arise to do so. Lacking this incentive and
without the array of counseling services available on most
campuses, Internet classes continue to suffer from drop-out

rates substantially above those of most traditional colleges. Only time will tell how successful technology will be in overcoming these disadvantages and whether it can do so at a cost universities can afford. For the moment, however, all the brave talk of rendering residential campuses obsolete seems definitely premature.

Whatever the Internet's impact turns out to be, it clearly offers important educational opportunities to countless working people, young housebound mothers, and other individuals who cannot readily come to campus. Already, more than 75 million adults receive some form of continuing education every year; the money spent annually on developing vocational skills alone amounts to more than $40 billion. Experts predict huge growth in the need for skill training on the part of corporate employees, especially in sectors heavily dependent on technology.[21] For such people, the Internet offers "just-in-time" courses for busy professionals who suddenly need some specialized instruction; easy access for workers who cannot leave their jobs; and big cost savings for companies accustomed to having to pay for travel, food, and lodging every time they send an employee away for training.

The opportunities for the Internet extend well beyond the United States. Vast numbers of potential students are now within reach of American higher education in countries that lack universities with the reputation or the resources of their leading counterparts in this country. Already, little-known universities, such as Liberty and Golden Gate, offer on-line courses to students throughout the world.

The potential market for distance education via the Internet seems so large that many commercial enterprises are beginning to regard it as a major opportunity. The University of Phoenix, founded as a for-profit, vocationally oriented university, managed to enroll 110,000 students by 2001, many of them on-line. Corporations are rapidly expanding their use of the Internet to train their employees. Publishing companies are planning to give far greater priority to educational activities, and consulting companies are doing the same. Hoping to strike it rich, other new firms besides U.Next have offered large sums to partner with leading universities to profit from the new technology.

Universities, too, are responding. Already, Duke University offers an on-line MBA to foreign students, while the University of Maryland provides Internet courses to students in many countries. Stanford and MIT, among other institutions, offer distance learning programs to companies whose engineers seek Master's degrees in rapidly advancing fields. Price-Waterhouse has formed a consortium of colleges to give on-line education to servicemen and women around the world. A. D. Little is organizing a group of business schools to develop Internet training courses for the Internal Revenue Service. Cornell has founded its own for-profit company.

There are even signs that universities are making serious efforts to experiment with new uses of technology that could lower costs and improve student learning. The Mellon Foundation, for example, has funded a series of efforts on different campuses to use the computer for educational purposes and to carefully assess the results. With the help of new technologies, institutions such as the Harvard Business School can now offer managers a full line of educational products, including courses for midcareer executives, here and abroad, some conducted largely by Internet; tailored programs created for particular companies; audiotapes of well-known faculty experts that busy executives can listen to on airplanes; and desktop "books" offering checklists of items that managers facing typical business decisions can review, with instant computer access to further readings for those who wish to pursue particular aspects of the problem in greater depth.

THE UNCERTAIN PROSPECTS OF THE INTERNET

These developments hold great promise for improving education throughout the entire university. The sheer expense of developing quality Internet instruction—estimated at up to $1 million for a single course—will force universities to think hard about how such offerings can be put together and presented most effectively. Besides, Internet courses, unlike traditional classes, are not the work of a single teacher; they require a team of up to twenty people: course designers ("content specialists"), writers, technicians, instructors, and others. The collaborative work of such a team in creating a finished product will itself provoke more discussion about pedagogic methods than teachers in a university normally experience. Many of the innovations used in such classes—including games, simulations, case studies, interactive software, and the like—can be adapted to improve traditional courses on campus. The competition generated by new suppliers, all struggling to appeal to the same markets, could well produce unprecedented efforts to use the new technology in valuable ways. Already, as distance learning shifts its emphasis from how to teach to how students learn, new firms entering the field are employing cognitive psychologists to help design courses and testing each segment with focus groups in a manner unknown to conventional college teaching.

Expanding the university's audience through the Internet could even help restore a healthier balance between teaching and research. One reason that so many professors have emphasized research over teaching is that research results can be widely read in the outside world, bringing prizes, fame, consulting opportunities, job offers, and many other rewards not available to the successful teacher, whose talents are seldom known beyond the campus. With the Internet, all this changes. Instructors online can attract far larger audiences than is possible with conventional classes. Successful teachers may even become celebrities, reaching audiences across the country and overseas. Their value to their university will increase. Observing their success, rival providers may bid for their services, raising their salaries far above traditional levels. Such rewards may in turn stimulate other faculty members to work harder at their teaching.

The question remains whether universities can best exploit these glittering opportunities by organizing their own on-line education on a profit-making basis. Columbia, the University of Chicago, and the other leading institutions that signed on with U.Next seem to think so. Clearly, this strategy has some advantages.[22] The prospect of making money will certainly give universities a powerful motive to make the most of the new medium. Since the costs of entering the field are high, the chance to share the risk by obtaining the necessary funds from other sources is very tempting. Setting up a for-profit company with outside funding may also make it easier to attract first-rate producers, technicians, and marketing executives by offering them an equity stake. Collaboration with professional investors may even help in finding the best business talent to make the new enterprise a financial success. And if the venture succeeds, of course, the university will earn substantial sums of money it can use to fund new fields of research, new educational programs, new scholarships, or any of a number of other worthwhile initiatives.

Not all faculty members, however, are celebrating the arrival of the Internet, especially when it is used to make a profit from education. To some, the new technology is just another way by which university officials can exploit the faculty. Gary Rhoades reports that "decisions [to use the Internet in teaching] increasingly bypass collective faculty control and are made with an eye toward efficiency and profit instead of educational quality."[23] According to York University's David Noble, citing examples from several institutions, the first step will be to assert ownership of all Internet instruction by the administration, followed by a requirement that professors put their teaching materials on-line.[24] Eventually, skilled actors may be used to deliver lectures and skilled technicians will convert them to Internet use. In this way, universities will transform their professors into hired hands and make them subordinate to producers and other authorities who exploit their labor and appropriate the profits.

As Noble describes it:

> Once the faculty and courses go on-line, administrators gain much greater direct control over faculty performance and course content than ever before, and the potential for administrative scrutiny, supervision, regimentation, discipline and even censorship increases. . . . The use of technology entails an inevitable extension of working time and an intensification of work as faculty struggle at all hours of the day and night to stay on top of the technology and respond, via chat rooms, virtual office hours, and e-mail to both students and administrators to whom

they have now become instantly and continuously accessible. The technology also allows for much more careful administrative monitoring of faculty availability, activities, and responsiveness.[25]

"At last," some readers will murmur approvingly, "a measure of accountability for the faculty"; "alas," others will reply, "1984 has arrived." In fact, Professor Noble's prediction seems plausible only in universities where the administration is indifferent to whether its professors stay or leave. At major universities—which are likely to be the only ones making money from the Internet—the situation promises to be radically different. Professors are the life-blood of these institutions. On the abilities of the faculty rests the capacity of the university to attract good students, obtain research grants, and maintain and improve its reputation for quality. Because able scholars can readily move to other institutions, the administration must treat them with great care. Presidents can be replaced much more easily than a first-rate faculty. Thus, a vote of no-confidence by the faculty is generally fatal to a president, and the departure of any significant number of highly regarded scholars is a matter of grave concern.

In these institutions, far from being exploited, senior faculty are likely to hold the whip-hand. Professors who teach subjects with commercial potential, such as business and engineering, will have opportunities to teach on-line for other providers at very high rates of pay. Administrators may try to prevent them from accepting these offers, but such restrictions are not likely to last for very long unless the institution can provide comparable opportunities of its own.

Universities that would not dare to exploit their tenured professors may nonetheless hire graduate students and part-time faculty at low rates of pay to grade papers from Internet students and answer questions on e-mail about course assignments. This practice has been common in teaching undergraduate courses; there is no reason not to expect it to occur in on-line programs as well.

Critics may denounce such behavior as exploitative, but not everyone will agree. Evidently, the graders and instructors involved would rather take the work than seek alternative employment. If the pay seems low, the root problem is probably that too many students have attempted to earn a Ph.D. Moreover, who is to say whether it would be better for the university to offer higher wages? After all, any money the institution earns from its on-line venture will not go to wealthy shareholders but may help to buy books, provide scholarships, or employ other scholars. Under these circumstances, charges of "exploitation" are difficult to prove.

If exploitation does occur, could students end up as the victims? Without doubt, the way to make money from Internet education is to build as large an audience as one can while keeping the incremental cost of each additional student as low as possible. In other words, use interesting and appealing lecturers, add attractive visuals, but give as little feedback and personal attention as one can get away with, since these services will entail further costs that will reduce, if not eliminate, any profit gained from enrolling additional students. Such calculations could result in courses presented in superficially attractive formats but with little of the active learning that educators consider most valuable for the student.[26]

Universities that launch for-profit Internet ventures will presumably deny that any exploitation of students will occur. After all, if one thing is certain, it is that competition in

Internet education will be fierce, with universities, consulting companies, corporations, and other for-profit institutions all vying for the business. Under these conditions, market enthusiasts predict that the largest rewards will go to the provider with the highest quality product. Good courses will drive out bad, and competition will ensure an intense effort to improve quality. Well-presented Internet classes with 24-hour-a-day interactivity will replace those large lecture courses and their sections of variable quality taught by inexperienced graduate students. Out of this competitive process, students could well emerge as the beneficiaries rather than the victims. Or so university spokespersons will argue.

Critics may still complain that competition, however effective, will ultimately cause the market to supplant the faculty as arbiter of what is taught and how it is communicated. True enough, but surely the students are entitled to some voice in determining what they learn, especially the more mature adults who will make up much of the audience for Internet education. Besides, what is the alternative? If universities do not enter the field, refusing to cater to consumer and vocational tastes, other providers, such as the University of Phoenix, will do the job for them, with even more blatantly commercial results. On the other hand, if universities compete, any profits they earn can presumably go to finance precisely those precious forms of teaching and research that cannot be supported by the marketplace alone.

One can understand, therefore, why universities might decide to enter the new world of Internet education to earn a profit. Their presidents and deans do not believe that they will take advantage of anyone or try to sell an inferior product. Nor are they deterred from launching such a commercial venture by the unfortunate example of intercollegiate athletics. Whatever else they may have done, college sports have certainly not harmed the quality of play; no one has ever accused big-time football of offering a shoddy product. The problem with athletics is that the "product" has nothing to do with the intellectual purposes of the university, with the result that excellent play is often achieved at the expense of the athletes' education and the academic standards of the institution. With Internet learning, why shouldn't competition work equally well to improve the product? And if it does, the product this time will not be ancillary to the main purpose of the institution but part and parcel of its academic mission. What's more, any profits earned can go to make the university's teaching and research even better. Could any rational person resist such a result?

6 | THE BENEFITS AND COSTS OF COMMERCIALIZATION

Commercialization typically begins when someone in the university finds an opportunity to make money: an offer of generous research funding in exchange for exclusive patent licensing rights; a chance to sell distance courses for a profit; or a lucrative contract with an apparel manufacturer offering cash and free athletic uniforms in return for having players display the corporate logo. University officials naturally welcome the prospect of new resources that can help them fund a promising program or close a looming deficit. They eagerly investigate the opportunity and calculate the returns it will bring. Only with these benefits in mind, do they start to give serious thought to whether the proposal raises serious risks to academic values. By this time, the dominant urge is to figure out how to organize the venture so as to contain the dangers, allow it to go forward and start the money flowing.

From the early days of college football to the recent growth of for-profit Internet ventures, this method of proceeding has repeatedly gotten universities into trouble. Occasionally, officials have found themselves trapped in the swamp of big-time college athletics or embroiled in a scandal arising from a conflict of interest involving research on human subjects. More often, the institution has simply allowed itself to weaken admissions standards slightly, or settle for cheaper, but lower quality, instruction, or tolerate a bit more secrecy in its laboratories. The record is sufficiently flawed to warrant reexamination. What benefits do commercial ventures bring to the academy, and how substantial are they likely to be? What are the risks and what does experience teach us about the subtler costs that commercialization can entail?

BENEFITS

Profits

The obvious attraction of most commercial ventures to their university sponsors is the prospect of bringing substantial new revenues to the university. In the hands of academic officials, such funds have the ennobling quality of being used, not to line the pockets of private investors, but to help fund scholarships, purchase library books, pay for new laboratory equipment, or support any one of a number of worthy educational purposes. Moreover, in contrast to many of the gifts, grants, and legislative appropriations that a university receives, commercial revenues have special value because they can generally be used for any purpose officials choose.

Despite their attractive features, commercial profits do not always live up to expectations. All too often, they fail to materialize in the hoped-for amounts. The history of athletics clearly shows how rising costs can eat up anticipated gains, leaving most institutions with modest returns, or even losses, along with millions of dollars squandered on stadiums and other expensive facilities that could have been better spent on education or research. Similar results have occurred in other commercial pursuits as well. Of an estimated 200 or more patent licensing offices on American campuses, only a small fraction received more than $10 million in 2000 and a large majority failed to earn any appreciable profit.* Attempts to strike it rich by investing in companies started by members of the faculty have likewise tended to produce disappointing returns. Although profit-making Internet ventures are too new to assess their ultimate profitability, early failures at institutions such as New York University and Temple, not to mention the travails of such for-profit ventures as Fathom and Pensare, suggest that much the same pattern will prevail in this new field as well.

Even if universities do make a profit, they may not keep it, at least in public institutions. Often, a visible surplus simply causes the legislature to reduce appropriations, thereby nullifying any positive effect on the academic budget. Moreover, any profits that do remain may well be used for questionable purposes. For example, surpluses from football and basketball typically pay for scholarships given to athletes in other sports, such as track or tennis or swimming, that cannot support themselves. Far from promoting academic pursuits, therefore, athletic revenues compound the problem by helping to underwrite even more students who would not qualify for admission under the normal academic criteria.

*The year 2000 was by far the best year ever for receipts from patent licensing. Universities reported more than $1 billion in earnings. Nineteen institutions received more than $10 million, but only approximately 50 reported receipts exceeding $2 million. See Goldie Blumenstyk, "Value of University Licenses on Patents Exceeded $1 Billion in 2000 Survey Finds," *The Chronicle of Higher Education* (March 5, 2000).

Incentives

At this point, readers may complain that the tone of the discussion has been too negative, ignoring many of the greatest benefits of commercialization. After all, big-time college sports have brought entertainment to untold millions of Americans. Patents and corporate collaborations have greatly improved the process of turning scientific discoveries into useful products and processes (which, let us be frank, is the principal reason why Americans allow billions of taxpayer dollars to flow from Washington each year into university laboratories). As for the Internet and the quickening interest of private investors in distance education, might not competition and the lure of profit be the only forces powerful enough to break through the thick crust of faculty inertia and bring about some real progress in university teaching and learning?

These are all fair questions. Without a doubt, apart from any money they bring, profits create incentives that can induce universities to behave in ways that benefit the public. Again, however, one must be cautious in counting these advantages. Although they sometimes materialize, they often prove illusory. The history of athletics is full of brave assertions about gains that rarely turn out to be real: bigger gifts from alumni, improvements in the quality of the student body, important educational opportunities for minorities, to mention only a few. Even in the case of research, there are still critics who question whether the growth of patenting on campus has enhanced or retarded scientific progress and its effects on productivity.[1]

At times, moreover, when benefits to the public do emerge from entrepreneurial ventures, one can legitimately ask whether profit-seeking by universities was truly necessary to bring about the positive results. For example, competition from rival institutions, including for-profit universities and other corporate providers, might suffice to force campus officials to work harder at providing new and better Internet courses without the added incentive of making a profit. Similarly, much of the excitement that intercollegiate athletic competition provides for students and for athletes also occurs at smaller colleges where sports are conducted without the luxury boxes, the athletic scholarships, and the high-pressure, all-consuming effort that big-time football and basketball now require. As for entertaining the public, athletic clubs and professional teams have satisfied the popular demand for sports in other countries. It was not inevitable that America should become the only nation where universities use their students to present athletic spectacles for profit at the cost of compromising academic standards.

It also bears repeating that the incentives of commercial competition do not always produce a beneficial outcome; they merely yield what the market wants. Training courses will be cheap and of indifferent quality if employers merely require their employees to provide them with a certificate of completion.[2] Profit-making in supplying distance education via the Internet will only bring optimal results if students are discerning enough to gravitate toward high-quality programs. As in commercial television, excellent programming rarely comes about unless the audience demands it.

At times, competition for profit can actually produce deplorable behavior. Rivals can become so anxious to win that they resort to unsavory, even unlawful methods. In higher education, the constant cheating in big-time athletic programs offers a depressing illustration. The withholding of negative information from experiments conducted by Harvard's Scheffer Tseng provides another.

These cautionary remarks could provoke a tart response from enterprising university presidents who are working hard to move their institutions into the higher reaches of the academic hierarchy. "Such high-minded arguments," they may declare, "are all very well for a former president of a university accustomed to a secure place in the academic firmament and buffered from misfortune by an endowment that approaches $20 billion. But how can other institutions without these assets hope to achieve greater eminence unless they can pursue every available opportunity to gain the resources that excellence invariably requires?"

This is a valid question. In higher education, the cards are stacked against any institution that lacks an established reputation and a lot of money. The best younger scholars and scientists usually go to institutions that already have strong faculties. Foundations and government funding agencies also give the bulk of their support to universities with the best-known professors. The ablest students likewise gravitate to universities with established reputations. In time, these students graduate and transform themselves with uncommon frequency into financially successful alumni who then support their alma mater with larger gifts than other institutions can normally obtain.

In all these ways the strongest universities tend to perpetuate themselves almost automatically. Success begets more success, which helps to explain why the list of top-rated universities in 2000 looks remarkably like a similar list in 1950 or even 1900. This process understandably frustrates university presidents who, in the best American tradition, want to lift their institutions to new heights and chafe at watching the so-called leading universities continue to prosper even when their leadership seems stodgy and unimaginative.

With the odds seemingly stacked against them, enterprising presidents may conclude that commercialization offers the best chance for a resourceful leader to break through the barriers of tradition and gain an advantage over more established rivals. Big-time athletics may hold many hazards and the odds of success may be slim, but how else can a lesser known university hope to acquire greater visibility, attract new donors, and lure talented students who might otherwise be unaware of the institution's existence? Perhaps only a few universities will make a substantial profit from the discoveries of their professors, but what better prospect exists for suddenly acquiring a big new pot of money to upgrade departments and attract outstanding professors? The Internet may not prove to be a bonanza, and other schools with more established reputations may have a brand-name advantage, but maybe, just maybe, these institutions will prove sufficiently sluggish to give a more aggressive university a head start that will ripen into a lasting competitive advantage.

It is hard to argue against this line of reasoning, as far as it goes. Although the rewards of commercialization are much more speculative than many enthusiasts acknowledge, the chances may still be good enough, compared with the alternatives, to make such a strategy seem attractive. The trouble with the argument is that it is not complete. To make a full evaluation, one must consider the costs of commercialization as well as its potential benefits.

COSTS

The costs are, if anything, more speculative and intangible than the rewards; seldom, if ever, can they be expressed in terms of money. More often, they have to do with the elusive world of values, and specifically, with the principles that ought to guide academic pursuits and thereby enhance their quality and meaning. Among the risks to these values posed by commercialization, the following are most important.

Undermining Academic Standards

Research universities are rarely, if ever, any better than their faculties. If they are to make their greatest contribution, therefore, it is imperative that they guard the integrity of their procedures for appointing and promoting professors. Those who are entrusted with such decisions should make them solely on the basis of the quality of the candidate's teaching, research, or other contributions to the academic purposes of the institution. They should not appoint professors because they can bring a lot of corporate funding or because they are working on a project that holds little scientific interest but promises to yield large commercial rewards. If universities do not honor this principle, the quality of their academic work will surely suffer and they will find it harder to recruit scientists and scholars of genuine distinction. Even the *appearance* of hiring professors for commercial reasons will lower the morale of the faculty and diminish the reputation of the university in the eyes of other scholars by suggesting that it is not committed to research and education of the highest quality.

Another important principle for selective universities is that all students should be admitted on grounds germane to the academic purposes of the institution: that is, on the basis of their capacity to benefit from the educational program, enhance the development of their fellow students, and serve the needs of society. If applicants can gain admission through their friendship with campus officials or for other reasons bearing no clear relation to the university's mission, the institution will not make its greatest possible educational contribution. Once students are enrolled, any grades they receive for academic work should reflect an honest, objective evaluation of their performance in mastering the material of the course. Obviously, if grades can be bought or sold or altered for other reasons, the outside world can no longer rely on transcripts, some students will gain an unfair advantage over others, and confidence in the institution will suffer.

Athletics pose the most obvious threat to these principles. Large numbers of students are admitted to colleges every year with the expectation that they will play on varsity teams. Often, they are recruited by the coaching staff and would not gain admission were it not for their athletic prowess, an ability having no evident connection with the true educational purposes of the institution. Such students frequently come to college for athletic rather than educational reasons, much like star quarterback Brian St. Pierre, who announced that he chose Boston College over Syracuse University, not because he admired the reputation of the B.C. faculty for good teaching but because he preferred the football coach's pro-style offense.

Once admissions standards are lowered to accommodate large numbers of athletes with academic abilities and interests well below the average for their class, further dangers arise. Schools wishing to keep their best players eligible will be tempted to create easier courses and simpler academic requirements. When especially talented athletes are at academic risk, pressures will arise to find some way of keeping them in school, sometimes to the point of actually altering their transcripts or ghostwriting their term papers. The awareness of such practices, of course, only adds to the cynicism of students and lowers the faculty's respect for the institution.

In addition to maintaining the integrity of the admissions process, universities should also make all other educational decisions to further the interests of students and society rather than to please a powerful trustee, fit the private convenience of faculty, or achieve other extraneous goals. This does not mean that educators have to shape their curricula to suit the wishes of their students or the views of public officials. Students often overemphasize vocational courses; officials sometimes overreact to transient political sentiments; and both groups lack the experience to know what subjects can be taught effectively and how the teaching can best be carried out. Thus, the university, through its faculty, must make the final decisions about matters of teaching and curriculum. Still, the aim in forming such judgments should always be to meet the legitimate needs of students and society and not to serve some other purpose.

Commercialization threatens this educational principle, because the profit motive shifts the focus from providing the best learning experience that available resources allow toward raising prices and cutting costs as much as possible without losing customers. Since most students are young and cannot readily compare how much they will benefit from the educational choices before them, well-known universities can trade on their reputation by giving cheaper courses to make more money. Such practices violate a commitment that every educational institution owes to its students.

In similar fashion, profit-seeking can lead universities to share their educational resources less widely than they should in order to earn a larger surplus for use elsewhere in the institution. For example, because continuing education programs are often used as profit centers, they rarely provide scholarships and hence are not accessible to many poor, but worthy, potential applicants. Similarly, business schools in search of profit may set such high tuitions for their executive education programs that managers from smaller companies cannot afford to attend.

Another educational cost that commercialization can incur has to do with the moral example such behavior gives to students and others in the academic community. Helping to develop virtue and build character have been central aims of education since the time of Plato and Aristotle. After years of neglect, universities everywhere have rediscovered the need to prepare their students to grapple with the moral dilemmas they will face in their personal and professional lives. In colleges and professional schools alike, courses on practical ethics are now a common feature of the curriculum.

Although classes of this kind can serve a valuable purpose, students will surely be less inclined to take them seriously if they perceive that the institution offering the courses compromises its own moral principles in order to win at football, sign a lucrative research contract, or earn a profit from Internet courses. In deciding how to lead their lives, undergraduates often learn more from the example of those in positions of authority than they do from lectures in a classroom. The most compelling moral examples any institution can give are ones that demonstrate a willingness to sacrifice immediate self-interest, if need be, for the sake of some higher principle. Conversely, the worst possible examples are those in which the institution, despite its high-minded pronouncements, does the reverse.

Commercialization can also touch the lives of college students in other questionable ways. Two entering freshmen made news in 2001 by becoming the first to persuade a corporation to pay all their college expenses in return for spreading the company's message among their fellow undergraduates. Others will surely try to emulate this example, leaving campuses to contend with the prospect of more and more students proselytizing for their corporate sponsors. Meanwhile, other undergraduates are selling their lecture notes to private companies that are openly seeking materials of this kind for use in preparing course "guides" to sell to other students. Presumably, college authorities will wish to place restrictions on activities of these kinds. But how can they do so convincingly if they themselves have accepted money in exchange for allowing companies to use the institution and its teaching for commercial gain?

The constant struggle for more resources can also obscure the larger message of a true liberal arts education—that there is more to life than making money. Competition for students has already caused many colleges to emphasize vocational programs at the expense of traditional majors while aggressively proclaiming to prospective students what their degrees will be worth in the marketplace. The importance of material values can only increase in the minds of students if universities repeatedly demonstrate by their own behavior that they are willing to ignore basic academic principles when they get in the way of the search for more resources.

The last fundamental academic value is a fidelity to the basic canons of scholarly and scientific inquiry. To achieve the best intellectual results, investigators must be able to pursue the subject of their choice and to express their findings freely without being penalized for their opinions. In return, they should conduct their research openly and share their methods and findings freely with their fellow scholars in order to further the work of everyone concerned to the greatest possible extent. They should likewise try to express their views as truthfully and objectively as possible. Of course, human beings lack the power to eliminate all bias from their work. Every faculty will have members whose writings are influenced, perhaps unwittingly, by a desire for popular acclaim or a position of influence in the university or the outside world. Nevertheless, in a community dedicated to the pursuit of truth and knowledge, professors must do their best to be accurate and objective, and the university should do what it can to minimize extraneous influences that could bias or distort their findings.

Commercialization can interfere with these canons of scientific inquiry in several important ways. Introducing opportunities for private gain threatens to divert at least some researchers from exploring more interesting and intellectually challenging problems. This possibility might conceivably be benign if the market were a reliable guide to the most promising subjects of research. It is theoretically possible for commercial motives to play a useful role in weaning first-rate intellects from a sterile preoccupation with scholastic puzzles, like the players in Hermann Hesse's *The Glass Bead Game*.[3] But profit does not play this role in the realm of basic research. Much commercially profitable research is trivial from a scientific point of view; witness the large sums spent trying to prove that one new drug is marginally different from existing substitutes. Conversely, the most important inquiries in science often involve questions no company will support because the answers take the form of general laws of nature that hold no special rewards for the enterprise that funds the research.

Just as academic institutions price their continuing education programs beyond the reach of many students in order to earn a greater profit, so also can they retard scientific progress in order to maximize their income. This is essentially what happens when universities delay sharing research materials with companies in an effort to obtain a larger share of any profits that the firms eventually make. Similarly, zealous campus officials can slow commercial applications and drive up prices of valuable products by granting exclusive patent licenses, where nonexclusive licenses would be feasible, merely to let the university share in any monopoly profits that the exclusive licensee manages to earn.

Corporate research support will also require the university to accept a certain amount of secrecy, as chapter 4 pointed out, since companies will naturally wish to avoid having valuable findings from the work they fund fall into the hands of competitors. From the standpoint of the university and of science itself, however, secrecy has several unfortunate results. It disrupts collegial relationships when professors cannot talk freely to other members of their department. It erodes trust, as members of scientific conferences wonder whether other participants are withholding information for commercial reasons. It promotes waste as scientists needlessly duplicate work that other investigators have already performed in secret for business reasons. Worst of all, secrecy may retard the course of science itself, since progress depends upon every researcher being able to build upon the findings of other investigators.

Apart from secrecy, academic scientists who get involved in commercial pursuits may also acquire financial interests that bias their research. Most researchers are convinced that material considerations could not possibly influence their judgment, although a large body of evidence suggests that such biases do occur. Thus, even conscientious investigators may acquire financial interests that influence their work. Without the university's intervention, these conflicts can easily multiply and create a significant threat to the objectivity of research.

Finally, industry funding will sometimes compromise the integrity of research because the stakes are so high. If the outcome of a professor's inquiry can discredit a hugely valuable drug or cast doubt on the products or the production methods of entire industries, temptations will naturally arise to try to influence the outcome. Companies threatened in this way may try to cultivate and reward "friendly" academic experts or actually intimidate academic scientists, such as Betty Dong and Nancy Olivieri, who are about to publish results damaging to their products. In either event the objectivity of university science will suffer, in appearance if not in reality.

Damaging the Academic Community

Commercialization can undermine collegiality and trust within academic communities by creating divisions and tensions that did not previously exist. Professors who work hard at their traditional academic tasks will resent the extra income earned by colleagues who start a new business or spend a lot of time consulting. Humanists will feel devalued. Conflicts will arise between faculty and administration over the proper division of patent royalties or the management of a business founded by a professor but partly funded by the university. Graduate students may accuse their supervisor of taking their ideas to benefit a company in which the professor has an interest. Scientists may bridle at the secrecy imposed by a colleague in their department who is funded by a corporation.

The way in which entrepreneurial universities treat academic values will also have subtle effects on the commitment of the faculty to the work of the institution. Presidents and deans have little coercive authority; they cannot order professors to teach better courses, or pay more attention to students, or labor longer at their research. They can succeed only through persuasion, and their power to persuade depends on their ability to win the loyalty and respect of their faculty colleagues. Such respect is far more likely to come through example than from words alone. Campus officials can hardly keep their professors from spending too much time earning money on the side if the university itself is trying to make a profit by investing in companies founded by its own scientists. Nor can presidents and deans expect their faculty members to refrain from selling their teaching services to Internet companies once the administration has joined with private investors in a for-profit distance learning venture.

Money is not the only cause of self-serving conduct on university campuses. Professors were known to exploit graduate students, shirk their collegial duties, and even refuse to talk about their research long before opportunities arose to make a profit from such behavior. But money adds another reason—and an especially potent one at that—for putting selfish interests and private pursuits above responsibilities to students and colleagues.

Such self-serving tendencies are particularly harmful to universities, since faculty members enjoy unusual freedom, and many of their most important activities cannot be prescribed in advance. Under these conditions, academic communities work well only when professors voluntarily choose to give generously of their time to help their institution, colleagues, and students. It is this willingness to do more for others than the job officially requires that is at particular risk in an age when able scientists and scholars have so many opportunities to seek fame and fortune in the outside world.

If universities continue to behave more and more like corporations by launching commercial ventures to enlarge their revenues, faculty members may reply in kind. Already, "faculty members not only are teaching less but have become less willing to serve on institutional committees, less willing to protect the institution from political disruption, and less careful to avoid exploiting the institution's name or facilities for economic gain."[4] Eventually, deans and presidents could find themselves discussing terms of employment, not directly with their best-known professors, but rather with professional agents who use the reputation of their faculty clients to negotiate lower teaching loads, off-scale salaries, and greater freedom to pursue lucrative outside activities. In similar fashion, graduate students and junior faculty, who have little power individually, may decide to protect their interests by forming unions and bargaining collectively with the administration.[5]

Risks to Reputation

Commercial activities can also damage the university's standing in the eyes of the public. Over the past forty years, confidence has declined sharply in the United States, not only in government but in all kinds of institutions, including universities. Significantly, the organizations and groups that still command greatest trust are invariably ones—such as the Supreme Court or the military—that seem most devoted to goals that are not self-serving. Universities have traditionally been thought to fall within this category, since they are dedicated to truth and understanding, and their professors earn much less than people of comparable intelligence and education typically receive in the private sector. Commercialization can eat away at this reputation, however, as word of its growing influence spreads from professional journals to congressional hearings, trade books, and even best selling novels, such as Le Carré's *The Constant Gardener.*

Universities have already grown more susceptible to public criticism because of their increased importance to society. When college and professional school become essential to coveted careers, students (and parents) are more inclined to feel resentful when they are denied admission or receive a failing grade. As universities grow richer, they begin to inspire envy more easily than affection. When campuses expand and acquire more land, they arouse greater hostility from the surrounding community. Amid these tensions, evidence of aggressive commercialism, and of the scandals and misadventures that often come in its wake, can easily provoke strong disapproval and distrust.

As trust declines, the risk of government intervention increases. Newspaper stories about the conflicts of interest of scientists performing experiments on human subjects or the money universities make on athletics through luxury boxes, television contracts, and advertising deals with clothing manufacturers create obvious opportunities for public officials to intervene. When Congress debates whether to act, universities that have openly indulged in entrepreneurial excess may find that the aura of public trust that once shielded them from hasty and unwise regulation is no longer available to protect them.

Of course, government intervention may be needed when there is no practical alternative. But regulation always comes at a cost, creating risks that unwise rules will result through political expediency, that red tape and needless delay will increase, that bureaucratic mistakes will proliferate. Already, officials are interfering more in the affairs of universities than they did in generations past in an effort to increase their accountability and their responsiveness to various constituencies. If the public comes to distrust universities more, and officials become even less inclined to respect academic autonomy, regulation may spread to such sensitive areas as admissions, faculty appointment procedures, curricular design, and other matters better left to academic discretion.

More important still, commercialization threatens to impair the university's reputation for objective, disinterested teaching and research. As medical schools grow careless in stopping pharmaceutical companies from manipulating the results of clinical tests, as professors keep writing articles on controversial subjects without disclosing their ties to interested companies, as deans allow advertising to accompany their teaching materials, the public may come to question the independence and impartiality of the institution and its faculty.

The university's reputation for scholarly integrity could well be the most costly casualty of all. A democratic society needs information about important questions that people can rely upon as reasonably objective and impartial. Universities have long been one of the principal sources of expert knowledge and informed opinion on a wide array of subjects ranging from science, technology, and medicine to economic policy, Supreme Court rulings, and environmental trends. This function has grown steadily more important now that so many issues that concern the public—biological warfare, global warming, nutrition, and genetic engineering—have become too technical for ordinary citizens to understand. Once the public begins to lose confidence in the objectivity of professors, the consequences extend far beyond the academic community. At a time when cynicism is so prevalent and the need for reliable information is so important, any damage to the reputation of universities, and to the integrity and objectivity of their scholars, weakens not only the academy but the functioning of our democratic, self-governing society. That is quite a price to pay for the limited, often exaggerated gains that commercialization brings to even the best-known institutions.

EVALUATING RISKS AND REWARDS

Looked at as a whole, the costs of increased commercialization seem considerably larger than the benefits. Yet weighing the advantages and disadvantages in a particular case often leads to a different conclusion. Such a process is not an exercise in scientific precision. Rather, it is much like asking whether an indeterminate number of olives, figs, and grapes should count more than an unknown quantity of apples, pears, and plums. The uncertainties involved cast a fog over the problem and invite personal bias into the calculations of those who make the decisions.

Evidence of bias is not hard to find. Looking back over the history of commercialization, one quickly perceives a persistent tendency to exaggerate the benefits and overlook or underestimate the dangers. Such a tendency is hardly surprising given the nature of the costs and benefits involved. The principal advantage to the institution—money—will usually seem immediate, tangible, and extremely useful to help meet pressing needs. In contrast, the dangers—to the conscientiousness of faculty, or to the moral education of students, or to the trust of the public—are all intangible and remote. They may never materialize, at least not for a long time, so that it is all too easy to overlook them.

In contrast to the rewards, which accrue directly to the institution, many important costs seem further diluted by the fact that they are not unique to the university but threaten values that each institution shares with all of higher education, such as public confidence in the integrity of academic experts or the free exchange of ideas among scientists. Most of these costs do not result from any one commercial venture but only emerge through the cumulative effect of many similar activities. As a result, when officials consider profit-making opportunities one by one, they have a natural tendency to ignore these cumulative risks. They may give little or no weight to the possibility that their decision to proceed will contribute, however slightly, to an erosion of public trust or to a growing willingness of faculty members to neglect their academic duties in order to spend more time giving paid lectures, consulting, or starting a new company. Officials know that any blame for turning down a potentially lucrative commercial proposal will rest squarely on themselves, while much of the cost that such a venture might entail will never be traced to any specific decision they make.

Not only is the usual method of evaluating commercial possibilities biased toward an affirmative outcome *within the decision-making institution*; a parallel bias exists *within the system of higher education as a whole.* As a number of separate universities become aware of similar opportunities—to accept commercial advertising in their Internet courses, for example, or to invest in companies started by their own professors—at least a few are likely to go ahead. Once these few move forward, others, in such a competitive environment, find it hard not to follow suit. Among a large number of independent institutions, each striving to better its position, the power of the minority to push other institutions into commercial activity is almost always greater than the majority's power to induce others to hold the line. Gradually, more and more universities will decide to commercialize, and as they alter their behavior, the standards for what is acceptable and unacceptable will begin to shift. Practices that were once universally condemned will now begin to seem tolerable. Another small step will have been taken in the steady advance of commercialization.

The record contains many instances of this process. Because of its long history, athletics is especially rich in pertinent examples. In considering applicants capable of playing on revenue-producing teams, admissions officers in colleges with high-powered programs have gradually allowed the qualifications and academic performance of admitted athletes to fall further and further below the level of their classmates. Meanwhile, rules about giving athletic scholarships, scheduling games that interfere with classes, limiting the length of seasons, and prohibiting freshman eligibility have been slowly chipped away in the interest of fielding better teams and increasing net revenues.

The same process seems to be occurring in the field of science research where earlier norms about limiting the use of exclusive patent licenses, lending research materials, refusing to invest in faculty-sponsored businesses, and avoiding secrecy have all been eroded in the hope of making money. In medical schools, pharmaceutical companies have gradually expanded their influence over the content of continuing education programs while gaining greater access to residents training in teaching hospitals. Experience with e-learning is much more limited, but there are early signs of a similar process. Once Columbia agreed to sign with a for-profit company, U.Next, other leading universities quickly agreed to follow suit.

Because of the biases inherent in the conventional methods for reviewing commercial ventures, universities need sturdier, more reliable safeguards if academic values are to be preserved. Analyzing commercial opportunities in the usual ad hoc way is virtually certain to result in a gradual decay of basic principles. What universities should do instead is to look at the process of commercialization whole, with all its benefits and risks, and then try to develop clear rules that are widely understood and conscientiously enforced. Without such rules, officials will find it all too easy to succumb to the lure of money, not because it is the proper path to take, but rather because it is the path of least resistance.

7 | REFORMING ATHLETICS

In 1987, after thirty-six years of service as the executive director and principal architect of the modern NCAA, Walter
Byers retired and began to write about his long career pre-
siding over intercollegiate athletics. One might have thought
that the resulting work would be another memoir rich in
anecdotes about the author's exploits and the famous sports
figures he had known. The book that finally emerged was
nothing of the kind. What Byers wrote was a lengthy indict-
ment of the entire system of big-time college sports, accus-
ing it of exploiting athletes in search of profit while pre-
tending to foster amateurism and educational values.[1] The
chief culprits in his view were college presidents and their
athletic directors, whom he roundly condemned for mouth-
ing hypocritical platitudes while resisting changes that would
make the system more honest and fair.

This was an extraordinary document from someone
widely regarded as the man chiefly responsible for the very
system he was denouncing. Chapter 3 has shown that Mr.
Byers was close to the mark in his criticism of the current
state of intercollegiate athletics. But was he correct in placing so much blame on college presidents? Or are these educators simply the helpless inheritors of a world they did not
make and cannot any longer change?

122   Many college presidents are aware, at least in a general way, of the price paid for big-time athletic programs. Nevertheless, most of them feel that they can do very little to improve matters. Acting unilaterally, they clearly lack the power to achieve significant reform; any serious steps in this direction would put their school at a severe competitive disadvantage and provoke intense opposition from sportswriters, boosters, (some) alumni, and even governors and legislators. The only conceivable course for a well-intentioned campus leader is to undertake the difficult, time-consuming task of persuading other college presidents to force the NCAA to enact stricter rules. For anyone burdened with all the other responsibilities of administering a university, this is not a course of action to be chosen lightly.

For a long time, pundits claimed that big-time athletics had lost its way because college presidents had carelessly allowed control of their programs to slip from their grasp into the hands of coaches and athletic directors. If only the presidents would assert themselves, it was said, they could put their house in order and preserve all the pageantry and fun of college sports without the cheating and academic compromises that are now such a familiar part of the game. In the 1990s, the presidents finally did assume greater control of the NCAA's Division I by giving ultimate authority over policy to a Presidents' Commission (now called the Board of Directors). And yet, the hoped-for reforms did not materialize. College sports continued pretty much unchanged, leaving the critics wondering why the presidents were not able to accomplish more.

If those in charge failed to act decisively, it was surely not from any lack of suggestions for how to do so. Mr. Byers recommended that presidents stop exploiting athletes and repeal many of the current rules that limit what they can earn and what they can do to better their economic position.

Others have gone even further and urged Division IA schools to treat their teams as professional clubs and negotiate salaries with their players.[2] Under this scheme, participating athletes would receive the compensation they deserve. They could attend classes if they chose, but universities would abandon the pretense that all their football and basketball players are really students attending college principally to learn and earn degrees.

Proposals of this kind have obvious attractions. They would put an end to the hypocritical talk about "student-athletes" and do away with the need to dilute admissions standards and academic requirements. They would also stop the use of the NCAA as a cartel to impose a (low) ceiling on the amount payable to athletes. This change in turn would remove much of the pressure to make under-the-table payments and resort to other shady tactics to attract and retain outstanding players.

Unfortunately, professionalizing intercollegiate athletics is actually quite impractical. With few universities managing to break even on their athletic programs, most institutions would find it difficult to pay more money to their football and basketball players without abandoning other sports that cannot attract enough revenue to cover their costs. The many schools that do not even make a profit from football and basketball would presumably have to opt out of the new system entirely and join another NCAA division.

These objections, however, are mere details. The real reason for rejecting this proposal is that it simply wouldn't work. Intercollegiate athletics cannot attract large revenues without sustaining the perception, valid or not, that the players really *are* students. Once this perception vanishes, the magic disappears. College teams become mere minor league clubs, few of which have ever won large public followings or elicited much interest from television audiences. Before long, the system would collapse, and university officials would have to acknowledge an uncomfortable truth. Educational institutions have absolutely no business operating farm systems for the benefit of the National Football League and the National Basketball Association.

OBSTACLES TO REFORM

If going professional isn't the answer, what *can* university presidents do to improve the current situation? Over the years, educators, sportswriters, and athletics officials have prescribed an assortment of remedies, many of which seem promising initially. Like professionalization, however, most of these reforms turn out to be much more problematic than their backers realize.

Some avenues to constructive change are blocked for legal reasons. For example, when the NCAA tried to restrain escalating costs by placing a cap on assistant coaches' salaries, the coaches went to court alleging that the cap amounted to an agreement in restraint of trade in violation of the antitrust laws. A federal court eventually agreed and entered a judgment of more than $50 million against the NCAA, thus putting a stop to cost-saving covenants of this kind.[3]

Another legal barrier has arisen as a result of Title IX of the Civil Rights Act, which requires universities to offer the same athletic opportunities to women as to men. Under this statute, each college must give a share of its athletic scholarships to female athletes that is roughly equal to the percentage of women students. Although the law has been beneficial overall, it has an unintended consequence. Because women do not play football, men have a huge advantage in the number of scholarships available in the revenue-producing sports. For this reason, colleges cannot restrict athletic scholarships to money-making sports and still comply with the law, even though the only convincing reason for giving such scholarships is to allow athletes who bring added revenue to their college to share in the receipts. Intercollegiate athletics would improve if universities could stop giving scholarships in the other sports; such a policy change would ease the financial pressure on the revenue-producing teams and lessen the power of coaches over the lives of student athletes. But Title IX makes this very difficult by forcing any school with a football team to award scholarships to women in nonrevenue sports, which in turn creates heavy pressure to do the same for men.

A number of other seemingly promising reforms turn out to be impossible, not for legal but for practical reasons. The pressure to win on the athletic field is so strong that member schools are likely to resort to widespread evasion of any rule that is not very clear and easy to enforce. Some years ago, for example, the NCAA passed a rule limiting the hours per week that athletes could practice their sport. With the connivance of coaches, however, athletes soon began to attend "voluntary" practices without formal supervision. The NCAA quickly learned that it could not enforce its limits effectively without planting spies on every member campus. Before long, the rule was a dead letter.

Similar problems have overtaken efforts to encourage athletes to work conscientiously at their studies. In pursuit of this goal, the NCAA has taken the seemingly sensible step of requiring all athletes to complete enough courses each year to make reasonable progress toward a degree. Those who fail to do so lose their eligibility to play. A number of colleges, however, have responded to the new rules by introducing majors in sports management and putting them under the control of their athletics department. Other colleges have created programs in "general studies," which enable athletes to take a random assortment of easy introductory courses and have them count toward a major in fulfillment of the requirements for graduation. Some established majors have been allowed to become safe havens for athletes of modest academic talent. Unless the NCAA undertakes the hopeless task of reviewing the academic content of each member college's courses, it is impossible to enforce the new rules effectively.*

Another obstacle to reform is the sheer difficulty of finding uniform rules that fit the widely varying circumstances of member institutions. The problems involved became apparent in 1983 when a group of presidents succeeded in drafting a rule preventing students with less than a 700 combined score on the SAT exam from participating in varsity sports during their freshman year. The authors of the rule were well-intentioned: they hoped to keep students who were academically at risk out of the pressure-cooker of varsity athletics until they had a year to establish themselves academically. As it happened, however, a 700 score was actually *above* the average for entering freshmen at a dozen or more member schools, so that students scoring close to that level could hardly be considered specially at risk. Conversely, the 700 cut-off was much too low to be meaningful at schools such as Stanford or Yale where even freshmen

---

*Much the same difficulty arises with respect to the recurrent proposals to replace athletic scholarships with financial aid based on need. The concept of "need" is not especially easy to apply, nor are departures from it always easy to identify. So long as the pressure to win remains extremely high, the job of policing all Division I schools to make sure that no one is "sweetening" aid offers to athletes would be immense.

with scores of 1000 would have been far below the median for their class and hence clearly on thin ice academically.

The obvious remedy would have been to tie the minimum to the average test scores of the entering class so that athletes with scores, say, more than 20 percent below the average for their class would be ineligible as freshmen. But this change would have placed put selective schools, such as Stanford, at a disadvantage in competing for athletes against much less selective conference rivals, such as Washington State. As a result, gaining agreement on a relative standard would have been very difficult.

Similar problems bedevil proposals for increasing graduation rates. Periodically, someone suggests that universities graduating fewer than a certain percentage of their players lose athletic scholarships or suffer some other penalty. Such proposals, however, affect different schools very differently. A university such as Stanford will have no difficulty meeting the goal, since its athletes have relatively strong academic credentials and the institution has a tradition of high graduation rates. Other colleges, however, may have many athletes with low academic potential and graduation rates for their entire student body that are below the recommended minimum. For these schools, the stipulated goals are much harder to meet and hence threaten to put them at a competitive disadvantage. If such a reform were enacted, such schools might respond by offering watered down courses and resorting to other evasive tactics in order to comply. In the end, the new rule could conceivably do more harm than good.

Faced with all these obstacles, most university presidents throw up their hands. Having many other problems to worry about, they abandon efforts at serious reform. Their response, though understandable, is unfortunate. Despite the roadblocks, presidents could still do a lot to minimize the harmful effects of big-time intercollegiate athletics even in the most visible, revenue-producing sports. The following possibilities are illustrative.

REFORMING HIGH-PROFILE DIVISION I SPORTS

One strategy for reform would be to introduce measures that strengthen the will to protect academic values and lessen the incentive to win at any price. A first step might be to have the Association of Governing Boards undertake a program to educate trustees about the effects of intercollegiate athletics on academic standards. This effort could be accompanied by agreements on the part of NCAA divisions or individual athletic conferences to require presidents to submit a report to their trustees every year setting forth a few basic facts, such as the SAT scores and high school rank in class of all freshmen receiving athletic scholarships; the grade averages of all athletes in the college; the graduation rates of athletes over the past few years; and the corresponding figures for the student body as a whole. Such reports might have little or no effect on some boards and some trustees. Still, reading the facts would counteract the widespread tendency to avoid the truth about big-time athletics while alerting college officials to gradually worsening trends. By putting the subject on the agenda each year and by highlighting the essential facts, the reports might focus attention on the problem and strengthen the resolve at least to prevent the existing situation from getting worse.

Presidents in Division I schools could take a stronger step by agreeing with members of their conference to phase in ways of sharing athletic revenues more equally so as to reduce the financial incentive to corrupt the system and corrode academic values. Eventually, bowl receipts, television revenues, and contracts with apparel manufacturers could all be divided among conference teams in equal portions. Division I presidents could go further and agree to distribute all of the net revenue they receive from basketball playoffs in equal amounts among the participating conferences.

Proposals of this kind may be dismissed as "impractical" and "naive," but it is unlikely that they would encounter much determined opposition from legislators, boosters, alumni, or other powerful constituencies. If presidents refuse to share, therefore, they cannot claim that they are powerless to act. Rather, they will signal that the only reforms they are truly prepared to accept are ones that do not cost them any money or deprive them of the (typically illusory) hope of somehow, someday striking it rich on the playing field.

Refusing to share would be unfortunate. The lavish financial rewards given to the most successful teams do not account for all the ills of intercollegiate sports by any means. Nevertheless, they strengthen the desire to win at any price that leads to periodic corruption, continued erosion of academic standards, more and more intense recruiting, greater and greater demands on the time and energy of athletes, and a pointless "arms race" of athletic expenditures from which no one really benefits. It is no coincidence that universities with major revenue-producing football and basketball programs have allowed much greater compromises with academic standards than those that exist in other sports and at other schools. Today, each victory in the Division I postseason basketball playoffs is worth more than three-quarters of a million dollars. As the amounts of money given to the most successful teams continue to escalate, the need to share these revenues to reduce their malign effects grows more urgent with every passing year.

Other reforms could try to ease the pressure of big-time sports on the academic work of the athletes. Colleges that award athletic scholarships could begin by negotiating with other members of their conference to amend the terms of these grants to remove the leverage they give coaches to exercise control over their athletes. Since 1973, scholarships have been awarded on a one-year basis. The net result is that athletes are under great financial pressure to do whatever it takes to retain their scholarship, even if the training schedule and other athletic demands make it difficult for them to get a good education or elect a demanding major. Under current rules, therefore, coaches have the power to require more time and effort from their players than are truly compatible with a full undergraduate education.

To alleviate this problem, universities would merely have to return to the practice prior to 1973 and agree to make a four-year scholarship commitment to the athletes they recruit so long as they remain in good academic standing. While such an arrangement would allow students to quit their teams for insubstantial reasons and still collect their scholarships, recruited athletes are almost always too wedded to their sport to take this step without provocation. By giving them the power to resist unreasonable demands without fear of financial loss, universities could do something to reduce the coaches' power to sacrifice the education of their athletes in order to win on the playing field.

The NCAA could do even more to improve incentives by not allowing athletic scholarships to revert to the team when players lose their awards for academic reasons. This simple measure would put more pressure on coaches not to recruit players who are at risk of academic failure. It would also give coaches more incentive to take a real interest in the education of their athletes.

Another useful step that Division I universities could take would be to eliminate freshman eligibility, at least in the high-pressure, revenue-producing sports. On academic grounds, there is no justification for taking freshmen, most of whom have academic credentials well below those of their classmates, and throwing them into a regime that requires thirty or forty hours of hard work per week, frequent trips that interfere with classes, and a single-minded concentration on sport that cannot help but detract from any serious effort to obtain an education.

The reason university officials usually give for their current policy is that keeping all freshmen off the field would be unfair to those athletes who are perfectly capable of carrying on their studies while playing their sport. But this argument did not prevent the NCAA from declaring freshmen ineligible for many decades, nor was it the real reason for abandoning the rule in the 1970s. A more likely explanation is that making entering students ineligible would incur the added expense of hiring coaches to guide freshman teams. Once again, therefore, money is at the bottom of dubious policies that colleges justify publicly on other, flimsier grounds.

Even the brightest freshmen would benefit from a year in which they could concentrate on their courses without having to meet the heavy demands of a varsity schedule. If concern for the academically capable athlete remains a problem, the NCAA could find various ways to get around the difficulty. Freshmen could be declared ineligible only for the high-pressure sports, such as football and basketball, where very few freshmen participants are academically strong. Alternatively, exceptions could be made for students with grades and scores above the average of the entering class. Such exemptions would not affect many student-athletes and would not put academically strong schools at a significant disadvantage vis-à-vis academically weaker members of their conference.

As a final measure, presidents in Division I conferences could agree on conference-wide rules designed to prevent athletic schedules from encroaching too far on students' academic work. Such agreements could prohibit midweek games that require athletes to miss classes. They could limit the length of seasons for certain sports. They could prohibit scheduling contests that take place during exams or within a few days before examinations begin. Such rules would not only help student-athletes receive a decent education; they would also signal to the entire institution that academic values are not completely subordinate to winning and making money.

OTHER SPORTS

Big-time football and basketball are so visible and so widely publicized that they obscure the fact that most college athletes—even at institutions of athletic renown, such as Michigan and UCLA—compete on other teams, such as swimming, track, and tennis, that rarely earn nearly enough to pay for themselves. These other sports offer far more scope for reform, because they seldom have strong vested interests capable of mounting overwhelming opposition to any substantial change in policy. As yet, however, universities have scarcely begun to capitalize on the possibilities for constructive action.

University presidents could take a helpful initial step by using their control over the NCAA to eliminate the pointless requirement that schools seeking Division IA status in football and basketball must field a minimum number of additional teams, complete with athletic scholarships and other undesirable features of professionalized intercollegiate athletics. There is no obvious reason why a college wishing to play at the highest level in one or two sports should need to pay the price of having to admit underqualified athletes, hire expensive coaches, give costly athletic scholarships, and lose a lot of money in a series of *other* sports. The real reason for the rule is to prevent universities from concentrating their athletic resources on a single sport, especially basketball, in order to gain Division I status, and thus share the money from the lucrative "March Madness" television receipts.* This objective is a poor excuse for a rule that wastes money and spreads professionalism. At the very least, the NCAA should think of other ways to restrict entry to Division I that do not have the obvious disadvantages of the current policy.

Still greater improvements would result if individual conferences agreed to abide by sound academic practices. Conferences could set appropriate thresholds for the grades and SAT scores of prospective athletes so that member schools could not stretch their admissions standards unduly to enroll highly talented players. Additional provisions could cover the scheduling of games to limit the length of seasons and minimize conflicts with class schedules and examination periods. Still others might diminish the professionalism and intensity of their athletic programs by limit-

---

*It is possible that the NCAA has also promoted this rule to show its concern for sports other than those that make money. If so, the requirement is a very poor way of making the point.

ing the size of coaching staffs and recruiting budgets and by prohibiting out-of-season practices.* Such agreements would entail little if any additional cost and hence should provoke much less opposition than similar pacts for the high-visibility sports, such as football and basketball.

COLLEGES OUTSIDE DIVISION I

The vast majority of American colleges do not belong to Division I but to Divisions II and III. Such schools do not have huge stadiums, nor are many of their games ever televised. Even in the major sports, teams in these Divisions may have devoted fans and enthusiastic student supporters, but they are rarely encumbered with the large booster organizations, fiercely loyal state legislators, and dependence on television revenues and ticket sales that combine to make reform so difficult in the big-time Division I schools.

A useful first step would be to end the practice of athletic scholarships, as Division III has long since done. The only persuasive justification for such generous aid is that athletes who help bring substantial revenue to their college deserve some compensation in return. Since even football and bas-

*Measures of this kind might help to counteract another worrisome trend: the tendency of athletes in many sports at all types of institutions (save Division IA public universities) to perform in the classroom at substantially lower levels than their prior grades and test scores would have predicted. Colleges generally have failed to pay sufficient attention to underperformance, not only for athletes but for blacks, Hispanics, and other categories of students who exhibit this tendency. As a result, no one knows exactly why athletes tend to perform below expectations when students heavily involved in other types of extracurricular activities seem to perform *above* anticipated levels. Since a central aim proclaimed by every college and university is to help its students "achieve their full potential," educators would seem duty-bound to investigate why athletes (and others) underperform and try to correct the problem.

ketball teams in Division II very rarely make money, this rationale has little force. To those who argue that athletes must spend long hours on the practice field (to the detriment of their studies), the obvious answer is not to compensate them, but rather to cut the practice time so as to interfere less with classroom demands.

Since Division III colleges have already forgone athletic scholarships, they may feel that their programs are sufficiently free of abuse to remove any need for reform. A closer look at the facts, however, should dispel such complacency. Because of their small size, many leading liberal arts Division III colleges have one-third or more of all students participating in varsity sports, a far greater percentage than at the big public universities. A substantial fraction of these students would not be admitted were it not for their athletic ability, especially in higher-profile sports such as football and basketball. The SAT gap between the high-profile male athletes and their classmates has grown significantly in recent years, according to Shulman and Bowen.[4] Large and rising proportions of athletes, even in these institutions, are now recruited by coaches and acknowledge that athletics rather than academic considerations played a major role in their decision about which college to attend. These are the characteristics most likely to be associated with an academic performance below the level predicted by SAT scores and high school grades. It is not surprising, then, that among the high-profile male athletes graduating in 1993 from Division III schools in the Shulman-Bowen study, 69 percent finished college in the bottom third of their class.[5]

These figures strongly suggest that every conference in Division III and Division II should examine itself with care and review the trends in its athletic policies and admissions practices over the past ten years or more to determine whether remedial action is in order. Wherever possible, conferences should seek agreements in all sports that drastically cut the number of students admitted for athletic reasons, establish minimum admissions requirements, stop giving coaches the power to decide which athletes to admit, make athletic schedules conform to academic needs, and reduce the size of coaching staffs and recruiting budgets.

Conference-wide agreements of this kind would not eliminate all the adverse effects of college athletics. Nevertheless, they would greatly restrict the damage, while setting an example that could ultimately put more pressure on Division I schools to reform. Of course, coaches would argue that other conferences that do not agree to curb the intensity of their programs will have an advantage in postseason championships. That is a small price to pay, however, for putting athletic programs on a healthier basis. A few athletes and their families might also object, but they will rarely be able to call upon outside constituencies powerful enough to block meaningful reform. In the end, then, there is nothing to prevent determined presidents from having their way.

All in all, therefore, Walter Byers was only half-wrong. He underestimated the difficulty of rescuing big-time sports from hypocrisy and exploitation, and his solution to the current mess seems impractical. But he was correct in refusing to let university officials off the hook by portraying them as helpless victims of a system they are powerless to change. Up to now, presidents have intervened only occasionally, usually when they have a proposal that promises to cost them very little and to leave no one at a competitive disadvantage. By every measure, the results have been less impressive than they should be. No one can expect presidents to accomplish the impossible. But their inability to halt the most deplorable practices of big-time football and basketball should not excuse them from doing what they reasonably can to limit the damage. Working together, they have the power, even in Division I schools, to carry out a number of meaningful reforms. They should move forthwith to take full advantage of their opportunities.

8 | PROTECTING THE INTEGRITY OF RESEARCH

In the early years of the twentieth century, professors debated whether they or their universities could properly obtain a patent and assert ownership over discoveries made in campus laboratories. Many eminent scientists frowned on the idea. Jacques Loeb of the Rockefeller Institute declared that "if the institutions of pure science go into the handling of patents I am afraid pure science will be doomed."[1] Johns Hopkins University rejected T. Brailsford Robertson as a candidate for a chair in Physiology because he had sought patent protection for his discovery of tethalin, even though he claimed to do so only to keep his idea from falling into corporate hands. The Rockefeller Foundation followed suit by threatening to stop funding Herbert Evans of the University of California, Berkeley, if he tried to benefit financially from his research by patenting a discovery made with Foundation support.

By the 1920s, opinion had shifted somewhat. Increasing numbers of academic scientists now believed that patenting might be permissible if all royalties went to their university. Harry Steenbock, for example, donated his exceptionally lucrative patent for irradiating milk to the University of Wisconsin, which used the proceeds to create a foundation to fund research.

The debate continued on into the 1970s, implicating two of the most important scientific breakthroughs of that decade. Herbert Boyer and Stanley Cohen first decided not to seek a patent on their discovery of a technique for splicing genes but eventually relented and gave the patent to Stanford University and the University of California, San Francisco, which proceeded to collect more than $150 million in royalties by 1996. On the other hand, Cesar Milstein and George Kohler, after discovering monoclonal antibody-producing hybridoma cells, rejected the very idea of obtaining a patent, arguing that it was inappropriate to control exclusive rights to a potentially life-saving discovery.

Congress ushered in a new era in 1980 when it passed the Bayh-Dole Act, permitting universities to patent discoveries made through research funded by the government. As universities established policies to take advantage of this dispensation, most of them agreed to share royalties with the inventor, apparently without encountering any protest on principle from the faculty. Not every scientist, however, embraced the new policy. For example, the eminent mathematician Norbert Wiener, founder of cybernetics, wrote in 1973 that treating ideas as property and introducing the profit motive of patent royalties instead of the pure love of discovery would "render sterile the soil of human intellect."[2]

Professor Wiener's view, uplifting as it seems, would have radical effects, since it could require putting an end to collecting royalties not only for scientific discoveries but for books written by members of the faculty. Professors are no more likely to agree to give up their book royalties than legislators, alumni, and other boosters are willing to give up big-time football. Nor is it clear that the world would be a better place if they did. Without the prospect of earning money, professors might be less inclined to write textbooks, while universities could well revert to where they were prior to 1980, making little or no effort to scour their labs to identify discoveries of potential value to society.

In any event, Congress has expressly decided, contrary to Dr. Weiner, that the public interest is best served by encouraging academic institutions to seek and license patents. The argument Congress accepted was that the prospect of earning royalties would make universities work harder to identify commercially promising discoveries in their laboratories. History seems to have vindicated this judgment.[3] Since Congress acted in 1980, many more research universities have instituted vigorous technology transfer programs and are seeking patents at many times the rate of previous years.

Unfortunately, in their zeal to bring more revenue to their universities, technology transfer officers have occasionally acted, especially in situations involving fundamental, early-stage discoveries, in ways that threaten to slow progress rather than promote it. For example, they have refused to share important research tools with other universities unless the latter agree to give them a share of any royalties eventually earned through inventions making use of the loaned materials. They have likewise given exclusive licenses to a single firm to develop basic discoveries well upstream from any eventual applications or useful products. By so doing, they have prevented a healthy competition to exploit the patented knowledge, hoping instead to have their university share in the monopolistic profits earned by the exclusive licensee.*

*These problems, together with appropriate remedies, have been ably discussed by Professor Arti K. Rai in a talk delivered to the Emory University Conference on the Commercialization of the University, April 6, 2002.

These excesses on the part of some institutions do not negate the value of Bayh-Dole in stimulating universities to work harder at technology transfer. They do reveal a need for corrective action to avoid particular practices that hold back rather than promote the progress that Congress was trying to achieve. One remedy would be for universities to agree not to use exclusive licenses or other restrictions on the sharing of early-stage discoveries with other researchers. Failing that, Congress could modify existing legislation to make it easier for the NIH to deny universities the right to grant exclusive licenses on patents received with the help of government funds when such licenses would tend to retard subsequent research and development.

Notwithstanding the special problems just described, the record offers scant support for Dr. Weiner's broader claim that the profit motive will divert researchers from more important forms of intellectual inquiry. Two decades of experience reveals no significant tendency to abandon basic research for more profitable kinds of applied or practical work. Nor could anyone observing the growing numbers of learned journals and scholarly books make a convincing case that serious scholarship has suffered from the temptation to write best-selling textbooks and other popular works. Thus far, at least, the urge for discovery and the desire for respect from worthy colleagues have been more than a match for the lure of making money.

Though differences of opinion remain, therefore, one can hardly fault universities for earning money from the discoveries in their laboratories. In seeking royalties, they are merely doing what the law allows and Congress clearly meant to encourage. Since there are plausible reasons to support the government's policy, any argument to the contrary should be taken up with Congress, not the universities.

SECRECY

Since 1980, the government's new patent policies and advances in genetics have led industry to seek closer ties with university scientists and offer much new funding for basic research. As chapter 4 pointed out, however, corporate money has come with demands for restrictions to guard the commercial interests of the sponsoring company. Properly limited, such restrictions may be warranted. Nevertheless, corporate demands are often so sweeping and so onerous that they compromise the openness and objectivity of academic science.

The first line of defense against these pressures is a clear set of policies and a vigilant office to review all research contracts and resist any provisions that would require excessive secrecy, inhibit informal conversation among colleagues, or permit the corporate sponsor to influence the findings of university investigators.[4] As the travails of Betty Dong and Nancy Olivieri make clear, universities cannot count on their professors to spot such restrictions and insist on their deletion. Professional help is needed from reviewing officials who understand that their job performance will be measured not merely by the amount of research money they process or by the returns from royalty provisions they negotiate, but also by their success in opposing any contract provision that impinges unduly on the freedom of investigators. Universities should stoutly resist any effort by a corporate sponsor either to restrict the informal interchange of ideas within their institution or to keep results secret for more than two or three months after the research has ended. They should oppose equally strongly any attempt by sponsoring firms to control the data, influence the design, or participate in writing up the results of any research project conducted by members of the university.

CONFLICTS OF INTEREST

Universities should likewise have clear rules governing conflicts of interest on the part of their investigators, especially when the research involves experiments on humans. Almost everyone agrees that limits of this kind are needed, but dispute continues over what the rules should contain. Is it enough to require that researchers disclose any conflicts they have, or should universities go further and keep them from doing any research for companies with which they have significant financial ties?

Merely reporting potential conflicts to the dean's office seems plainly insufficient. University officials are often reluctant to anger influential faculty members and hence can be too permissive in reviewing financial conflicts, especially when they involve lucrative consulting arrangements or valuable investments owned by prominent professors. Asking scientists to send periodic reports to an overburdened university staff is no better; such a policy does not even guarantee that conflicts will be disclosed to human subjects participating in tests of new drugs or to readers studying papers in professional journals. One study of the ten medical schools receiving the largest amounts of federal funding found that only two required investigators to reveal financial conflicts to human subjects in clinical tests.[5] Another survey reviewed the contents of journals that ostensibly required disclosure of financial conflicts and found that, in fact, articles almost never revealed the author's financial ties to interested corporations even when the ties were substantial.[6] Two-thirds of these journals did not contain so much as a single disclosure of financial conflicts during the entire year (1997) of the study, presumably because no one had informed them that such conflicts existed. Such findings strongly suggest that many routine reports of financial ties never go beyond the university bureaucracy to alert patients, scholarly publications, and others with a clear interest in knowing the facts.

A stricter approach would require every investigator with significant conflicts to disclose the information to human subjects before they agree to participate in a test. Such a rule would ensure that those with the clearest need to know would be informed of the relevant facts. Yet requirements of this kind present problems. Officials often do not know whether researchers have explained the conflict clearly enough to prospective subjects in a clinical trial or whether the latter truly understand the risks involved. If the subjects are patients who are asked to participate in testing a new drug for cancer or AIDS, they may be too frightened and too dependent on the doctor involved to evaluate the conflict objectively.

These drawbacks suggest that requiring disclosure is insufficient and that universities should flatly prohibit their scientists from performing research on human subjects if the work is supported by companies in which the researchers have significant financial interests, whether from consulting arrangements, gifts, retainers, or stockholdings.*

---

*Exceptions might justifiably be made on rare occasions where the inventor of a new device or treatment possesses special knowledge that makes him (her) uniquely capable of carrying out clinical tests. In these cases, the university would need to take special measures to guard against the risk of bias.

Such financial ties do not merely threaten the integrity of the investigator; they may endanger the health and safety of patients. If something goes wrong and patients suffer, the reputation of the institution will surely be damaged. Under such circumstances, the university has a right to insist on rules that are effective enough to protect these interests.

Conflicts can also arise from research that does not involve human subjects when faculty members publish views on global warming, nutrition, or other controversial subjects with the help of funding from a company with a clear interest in these issues. The authors involved may be scientists, economists, or even ethicists (who are often funded by pharmaceutical firms while regularly speaking out on issues that could affect the commercial interests of their sponsors). An isolated grant from industry may not pose a significant threat to the integrity of the research. But problems arise if the investigator involved repeatedly receives such support or has consulting agreements or other substantial financial links with the companies involved. Such ties—or simply the hope of continued industry support—may exert a subtle influence on research or encourage investigators to continue publicly advocating positions helpful to their donors.

What universities should do in such cases is to insist that professors with substantial and continuing ties to any organization with an interest in the results disclose the nature of those ties or funding sources in any publications or official testimony containing their views.* Faculty members may

---

*In addition, universities should certainly require their researchers to disclose any significant financial conflicts to any individuals or organizations to which they apply for funds. For example, investigators soliciting support for a project involving a company in which they hold a substantial amount of stock should be required to inform the potential funder of the conflict.

protest, fearing that such disclosure will unfairly cast doubt on the credibility of their work. Arguments that the public cannot be trusted with the truth, however, are always suspect; readers may have good reason to be suspicious of opinions voiced by authors with a financial stake in the outcome. If no disclosure is made, moreover, and word later spreads about the conflicts of interest involved, the revelations may shake the public's confidence in the objectivity of *all* academic research, with resulting harm to the university's reputation and that of all academic scientists and scholars. These dangers surely give the institution good grounds for requiring disclosure of significant conflicting financial interests.

Harder questions arise in deciding whether a university should go further and prohibit investigators from proceeding with their research whenever they have substantial conflicts of interest that could affect their impartiality. Academic officials could claim with some reason that work carried out under such conditions carries a significant risk of bias that could jeopardize the institution's reputation for credible research. Arguably, disclosure cannot cure this problem; in fact, repeated disclosures of financial conflicts may deepen the public's suspicions about the objectivity of academic research and thereby place universities and their scientists and scholars under a cloud.*

While these concerns are legitimate, professors may re-

---

*Note that public officials with financial interests must sell their holdings or withdraw from any proceedings if a conflict arises. Still, a difference is that officials are making decisions that directly affect people's lives; professors who speak out on public issues are only expressing opinions that can be rebutted or discounted by an audience that is adequately informed of the facts. If professors do happen to do research that requires them to make decisions affecting patients or other individuals, they should presumably be held to the same conflict of interest rules as those normally applicable to other decision-makers in the public arena.

spond that forcing them to sell stock, break off consulting arrangements, or refuse funding from interested sources in order to conduct their research represents an unwarranted invasion of their academic freedom. Such restraints may be justified to protect human subjects. For other forms of research, however, the free marketplace of ideas can be relied upon to counter any problems of bias, especially if researchers are required to put readers on notice by disclosing any financial ties that might cast doubt on their objectivity. Although the university may worry about its reputation for credible research, reputational interests by themselves have never been enough to allow a university to discourage the free expression of views, even though faculty members periodically say things that provoke widespread disapproval and embarrass their colleagues and their institution. Similarly, universities cannot prevent professors from publishing merely because they have close ties with some organization, whether the Communist Party or religious groups that could plausibly bias their work. In all these cases, absent some immediate threat to other people, academic freedom prevails because of a faith that an open exchange of ideas provides the best defense against biased or misleading statements.[7] Faculty members can make a strong case that similar reasoning should bar their university from trying to avoid conflicts of interest by placing such sweeping restrictions on their ability to carry out research.

Any university that tries to impose such restraints may also find itself wading quickly into treacherous waters. For example, it would be arbitrary simply to prohibit financial ties with corporations; other kinds of relationships can create similar risks. Professors who regularly consult with the Pentagon, and who value this relationship highly, may feel constrained not to take public positions at variance with prevailing military policy. Faculty members who periodically seek funding from a large foundation may be reluctant to express conclusions that contradict strongly held policy views of the foundation staff. Once universities begin to grapple with such cases, they may soon be forced to make increasingly fine distinctions and to draw arbitrary lines that will inhibit the work of their professors and create much controversy and resentment among the faculty. Where no human subjects are involved, disclosure requirements should discourage enough serious conflicts of interest to allow academic officials to avoid having to confront such contentious problems.

Professors are not the only members of the university with questionable conflicts of interest. Academic institutions themselves can acquire financial ties of a troublesome sort. For example, universities, their affiliated hospitals, or even their departments and research institutes may hold a beneficial interest in substantial blocks of stock in companies for which the institution's faculty are conducting clinical research. If the holdings are a relatively small fraction of a much larger diversified portfolio, no conflict worth worrying about will arise. But if the holding makes up a substantial part of the assets supporting the university, faculty, hospital, or other unit in which the research is carried on, and if the outcome of the research could substantially affect its value, the possibility of conflict arises. The more important the holding is to the financial well-being of the academic unit and the greater the potential impact of the research on the holding's value, the more serious the conflict becomes. In appearance, if not in fact, a risk arises that the institution may exert subtle pressure on the design or the conduct of the research to benefit itself financially. If the conflict is substantial (i.e., if the potential gain to the academic unit is significant enough), it is normally best to dispose of the stock or to refuse to do the research in order to remove any perception of impropriety. In unusual cases where the research involved cannot be carried out nearly as well at any other institution, the university or the hospital should make full disclosure and appoint some sort of outside monitoring body that will review the research design and the data to ensure an objective result.[8]

A similar problem arises from the consortia that several medical schools have created to bid for contracts with pharmaceutical firms to perform tests on new drugs. Often, the primary reason for seeking such contracts is to make money, since drug testing is potentially lucrative but usually of little scientific interest. Having accepted such profitable work, however, universities and their laboratories have a strong financial incentive to maintain good relations with the companies involved. As a result, the university's commercial interests are in conflict with its responsibility to reach honest, objective results, however harmful they may be to the sponsor's bottom line. The risks created by such conflicts are not fanciful; investigators have shown that clinical trials supported by industry are much more likely to arrive at conclusions favorable to their sponsors than independently funded work on the same drugs.[9]

Even if no risk of bias existed, universities would be open to question for entering into contracts to use their valuable facilities and highly trained personnel for work that rarely has real scientific importance. Only a small percentage of clinical testing has any prospect of making a genuine scientific advance or even contributing to a truly unique product. Most testing involves "copycat" drugs that differ only slightly from products already on the market or minor variations on the sponsor's current drugs that it develops to extend its exclusive rights before its lucrative patents expire.

Such work hardly merits the risk of doing biased research. Medical schools would be well advised, therefore, not to enter into these profit-making arrangements and to carry out such investigations only when they are independently funded or done at cost for valid scientific or educational reasons as part of a faculty member's regular program of teaching or research.

EXCESSIVE RELIANCE ON INDUSTRY SUPPORT

A few universities have incurred another kind of risk by contracting with particular companies for grants large enough to constitute a substantial fraction of the total research budget of an entire department or academic unit. In 1998, for example, the Novartis Company agreed to give the Department of Plant and Microbial Biology at the University of California, Berkeley, the sum of $25 million over five years, a figure amounting to approximately 30–40 percent of the department's entire research budget. According to the agreement, Novartis gained the right to review in advance all proposed publications based on research supported by the company (or by the federal government) and to ask the university to apply for a patent on any findings contained in the research. The company not only reserved first rights to negotiate for a license on any patents resulting from the research; it also received two of the five seats on the committee to decide how to distribute its research funds.[10]

An obvious worry was that the Novartis contract would give the sponsoring firm too much power over the research agenda of the department. University officials dismissed this danger, however, pointing out that the faculty retained a majority of seats on the committee awarding the funds.

After three years of experience under the agreement, scientists in the department insisted that the company had not attempted to influence in any way the nature of their research.[11]

In isolation, the Novartis contract is probably not a significant threat to academic values. Presumably, the company agreed to give such substantial support because it believed that the work being carried on within the department had high commercial potential. As a result, the company would have little reason to alter the research plans of the scientists involved during the life of the agreement even if it had the power to do so. Nor would Novartis have had much chance of success if it had tried to exert influence. The department's scientists are under no obligation to obtain their funding from Novartis and are good enough that they could readily turn to other sources rather than adapt their work to suit the company's priorities. The university is also strong enough to resist such pressure, and its prominence makes the risk of adverse publicity very real to any company seeking to influence the department's work. Besides, the Berkeley faculty is only one of several excellent programs in plant biology. As a result, any arrangement it makes with Novartis will not pose much danger to the progress of science as a whole.

More serious problems would arise, however, if arrangements of this kind began to become widespread. Even if the sponsoring company had no seats at all on the committee allocating the funds, the hope of having such a generous agreement renewed could easily cause a department to be excessively responsive to the company's wishes about the type of research to be performed. University officials, anxious to retain the overhead from such substantial grants, might also exert quiet influence to keep the corporate sponsors happy. Although the most eminent departments could successfully resist such pressures, weaker departments might well succumb in various ways and begin to shape their research agenda to fit the company's priorities. In addition, the growth of similar funding arrangements (and especially the provisions granting the corporate sponsor preferred access to results from work done with government support) would give such companies an unfair competitive advantage over smaller rivals that could not afford to make multimillion dollar research grants to universities. Even so, the likelihood of many more agreements of this kind seems small, since similar contracts have rarely proved beneficial to the firm involved on the few occasions when they have been tried. Even so, the Novartis agreement is a dubious precedent that should be watched and actively discouraged if the practice begins to spread.

INVESTING IN FACULTY ENTERPRISES

A final practice raising problems for academic science is the investment by universities in companies started by their own faculty members. Twenty years ago, academic officials seemed reluctant to take this step.[12] Before long, however, they found the temptation to make a financial killing on the work of their professors irresistible. Aware of the criticisms such investments might provoke, most institutions created buffer organizations of some kind that were ultimately controlled by the university but removed from the direct supervision of anyone with authority over the professors in whose companies the university was investing.

Holdings of this kind cause a number of problems. They create the possibility of conflict between the university and its professors over the management of companies in which both have financial interests. They put the institution in the awkward position of having to pick and choose among its own scientists—perhaps even supporting some that are directly competing with companies founded by colleagues. By investing, universities implicitly endorse such business ventures and thus encourage faculty members to spend more time than they should on entrepreneurial activity. If academic institutions hold a substantial interest in a professor's company, they may also incur a certain responsibility—or at least be held responsible by the public—for any harm the enterprise does by its product, its pricing, or its other policies. Worst of all, universities with a financial stake in the work of their professors may be influenced, or may be thought to be influenced, by commercial considerations rather than academic merit when they decide on promotions, salaries, or other sensitive personnel questions. Since the integrity of these decisions is so important, any risk of this type should be a matter of serious concern.

University officials obviously feel that they have disposed of these problems satisfactorily by establishing buffer organizations to make the investment decisions. Undoubtedly, such intermediaries help. Even so, anyone who knows the facts will be aware that the university still controls the investments. As a result, some risk remains that the appointments process may be subject, or appear to be subject, to commercial considerations. Moreover, faculty members spending too much time developing their own companies will still feel vindicated by the knowledge that their own university is supporting such activity.

Reasonable people can differ over just how serious these problems are. Still, one has to wonder whether the economic gains or the advantages to society justify the risks. In making such investments, universities may benefit from firsthand knowledge about the work in their laboratories but they may also be biased in favor of their own scientists or reluctant to turn down a faculty member whom they fear could move elsewhere. Moreover, investing in start-up companies is not a business in which universities have special expertise; it is doubtful that they can do a better job than experienced venture capital firms. Carnegie-Mellon may have made millions developing the Lycos Company, but other institutions have not done nearly so well. Harvard's venture firm, which was amply supported by outside investors, closed down after a few years having made only meager returns. Accounts of similar attempts by other universities are not much more promising. After reviewing the record of these investments, Josh Lerner recently concluded that "case studies and empirical evidence raise serious questions about whether such efforts are likely to be sustainable. Rather than entering into these treacherous waters, university technology transfer officials and administrators may be better served by investing in developing strong relationships with the venture capital community."[13] All in all, it seems doubtful that the prospective rewards from these investments are worth the risk of compromising academic values.

DRAWING THE LINE

Modern science does not permit any neat division between industrial and academic research. As Rikard Stankiewicz has observed, "Modern technology has reached a degree of intellectual sophistication which makes its institutional separation from science counterproductive for both."[14] For this reason, public policy actively supports collaboration between the two sectors. Such a policy deserves respect, since most of the scientific research carried on in university labs is funded by public dollars.

Yet closer ties between university science and industry create all sorts of risks for compromising the openness, objectivity, and independence of academic research. Along this hazardous terrain, many universities have chosen to inch their way, step-by-step, anxious to maintain as much freedom of maneuver as they can and ever hopeful of somehow managing to have their cake and eat it too. This course of action is dangerous. When rules are unclear and always subject to negotiation, money will prevail over principle much of the time. Resourceful companies will pick universities apart, finding individual faculties willing to grant them what they want, then using these concessions to pressure other institutions with which they seek to interact.

Academic leaders do not need to run these risks. Enough experience has accumulated by now to draw adequate lines that will allow a vigorous technology transfer program but preserve the openness, independence, and objectivity that good science requires. It is unhealthy for universities to have their integrity questioned repeatedly by reports of excessive secrecy, conflicts of interest, and corporate efforts to manipulate and suppress research. Surely the time is ripe to set appropriate limits and see to it that they are vigorously enforced.

9 | PRESERVING EDUCATIONAL VALUES

In the turbulent world of public education, a battle is in progress over the role of private enterprise in reviving troubled urban schools. For-profit companies, such as the Edison Corporation, are bidding to take over individual schools or even entire city systems, claiming that they can raise test scores, instill a new spirit of learning, and still make money in the process. Teachers' unions have fought back strongly, arguing that educators driven by the bottom line will not have the students' best interests at heart. To the National Education Association, the selfish motives of business executives are no substitute for the single-minded concern for young people that first-rate education requires.

In recent years, this debate has spilled over into the less contentious domain of higher education. Articles have regularly appeared inquiring whether for-profit universities will eventually make deep inroads into what has long been the exclusive preserve of nonprofit colleges and universities. Analysts watching the rapid growth of the University of Phoenix ask themselves whether they are looking upon the future of American higher education. Established corporations and entrepreneurs alike see a huge and growing market for advanced education powered by the burgeoning demands of a corporate sector struggling to adapt to an ever more complicated, technologically driven environment. Looking further, they find the world of higher education dominated by large, self-satisfied universities: inefficient, resistant to change, and overly indulgent toward pampered professors who seem largely unaccountable to the students they supposedly serve. Viewed in this light, the vast, lucrative field of advanced education looks like the next health care industry, inviting incursions by enterprising businesses, confident that they can deliver what their customers want. To corporate investors, there is no apparent reason why the profit motive should not produce the same good results in higher education as it has in supplying countless other services that Americans need.

Like teachers' unions, educators at the college and university level tend to look askance at for-profit enterprises, questioning their ability to serve the true needs of their students. Curiously, however, as noted in chapter 5, universities have not been averse to operating some of their own programs at a profit, whether they be continuing education courses, executive programs for business, or (in days gone by) correspondence schools for those unable to come to campus. Perhaps academic officials think the profits they make are somehow purified by the worthy ends to which they will be put, in contrast to commercial profits, which merely fill the pockets of wealthy stockholders. Whatever the reason, this seeming inconsistency appears to have gone unnoticed and unexplained.

The debate over schools and universities raises deeper questions about the appropriate role of profits and private enterprise in higher education. Can commercial firms ever serve a useful purpose in this field? If so, what conditions must prevail in order to take the energy and initiative fueled by selfish motives and direct them toward useful educational ends?

THE ROLE OF PROFITS

To explore this subject, one must begin by distinguishing between competition and profit as sources of motivation in human affairs. *Competition* occurs when a number of actors vie with one another to reach a goal they cannot all achieve in equal measure. The goal can be anything human beings covet: money, fame, respect, even marriage. The knowledge that some will do better than others gives an incentive to excel, to do one's very best. The strength of the incentive depends on how much the goal matters to the competitors. *Profit* is simply one goal among others to which competitors may direct their efforts. Because many people put a high value on material wealth, however, profit often gives a powerful motive to succeed that generates much energy and ingenuity on the part of commercial rivals.

Although traditional universities are not organized to make a profit, they do compete vigorously with one another. Their goals are varied: to attract the best students, win Nobel prizes, defeat opponents on the football field. Their most comprehensive objective, however, is academic distinction, or prestige—an elusive concept that embraces the quality of the students and the scholarly and scientific reputations of the faculty. It finds its most concrete expression in the periodic ratings in publications such as *U.S. News and World Report* that rank hundreds of colleges and professional schools throughout the United States. Although the unreliability of these ratings is notorious, they continue to have an influence, since nothing else has been devised that provides such regular, seemingly exact measures of comparative academic quality.

Although universities work hard to improve their reputation, they are widely accused of emphasizing research over teaching to the detriment of their students. Commentators constantly criticize even the best-known institutions for this weakness, citing overly large classes, light teaching loads, dull lectures, heavy use of inexperienced graduate students, and refusals to give tenure to successful teachers. While some of these criticisms are overdrawn, few knowledgeable observers would deny that research universities rarely insist on the best possible teaching or make a sustained and systematic effort to improve the quality of their educational programs.

If universities truly compete with one another, why do they neglect their teaching so? At least part of the explanation is that rewards for excellent research far exceed those available for excellent teaching. Successful scientists gain worldwide reputations. They receive abundant recognition, awards and prizes, opportunities to consult, offers from other institutions, and salary increases to counter these offers. In contrast, the successful teacher is often unknown beyond her own campus. Her rewards are limited to the satisfaction of a job well done and the gratitude and approbation of her students—all pleasures well worth having but seldom comparable to the fame and other, more tangible benefits given to the accomplished researcher. Small wonder that so many professors concentrate more on research than on teaching.

If students could easily find out which colleges and professional schools would teach them the most (and if they were sensible enough to make these findings a decisive factor in their choice of schools to attend), the outcome might be different. Suppose that *U.S. News and World Report* discovered a reliable method for measuring how much students learned in each college and professional school and began publishing their rankings on this basis. Soon, students would start to gravitate to the most effective schools. Presidents and trustees in other institutions would quickly notice that the ratings of their university had gone down and that the quality of their entering classes was declining. Faculty members would also perceive that the best students were beginning to go elsewhere. Before long, pressure would build to increase the effectiveness of teaching and learning, and professors who were demonstrably successful in the classroom would begin to receive handsome pay increases and other forms of recognition.

The actual situation on university campuses today, of course, is a far cry from the one just described. No reliable method yet exists that allows students to determine where they will learn the most. Since applicants are generally hard-put to know just how much they are really learning, let alone how much they can expect to learn at a school they have never seen, they do not make enlightened choices. They rarely possess either the time or the information to explore all the promising options available to them and usually have only a limited basis for comparing the options they do consider. Under these conditions, competition does not necessarily cause good instruction to drive out bad. Instead, students often flock to courses with superficial appeal or to institutions with established reputations even though the education they receive is only mediocre. Professors who work hard at their teaching and do a first-rate job of helping their students learn cannot count on receiving higher salaries in return; nor can their institutions assume that excellent teaching will attract better students and greater tuition revenues. Since success brings so few rewards, competition does not inspire universities or their faculties to do as much as they might to improve their instruction in the way that it forces computer companies to work at improving their products.

Could the profit motive somehow overcome this impasse and achieve a superior quality of education? Not necessarily. Although profits provide a potent incentive, the incentive does not always produce results of the highest quality. What it does is to give customers what they want. The two may not be the same. For the profit motive to produce the best possible education, three conditions must be met. Students have to know what they really need. They must be able to evaluate the available alternatives and make reliable choices. Finally, their preferences must correspond reasonably well with the needs of the society, since one important purpose of education is to prepare people to contribute effectively to the common welfare.

If any of these conditions is not fulfilled, the profit motive may not work especially well. For example, college students are widely thought to exaggerate the importance of vocational training and to underestimate the subtler values of a liberal arts education. If so, the profit motive will not compensate for this mistake but will give undergraduates all the vocational preparation they want to the neglect of other instruction that serves broader social needs, such as learning how to make sound ethical choices or how to play a constructive role as citizens in a democracy. Similarly, if teachers are routinely promoted simply for earning advanced credits, regardless of how much they have actually learned, they will not seek the best training but will flock to inexpensive courses of indifferent quality that many schools of education offer at a profit.[1]

Finally, because applicants know so little about the true quality of teaching and learning in the educational programs they consider, for-profit providers may try to attract them by offering superficially appealing gimmicks or by linking themselves to institutions with well-known brand names that may or may not offer excellent teaching. (The latter tactic explains why for-profit Internet ventures have made such efforts to sign up well-known universities as visible partners in distance education.) In either case, the resulting courses may not provide the highest quality of education.

The reservations just expressed do not mean that the profit motive can never be an effective force for improving the quality of university programs. They do suggest some important criteria to use in evaluating for-profit teaching ventures, whether they take the form of new commercial firms or existing university programs for executives. By and large, profit-seeking can have beneficial results for education when many providers compete vigorously with one another and when students know their needs and understand how well the available providers can fulfill them. It is worth asking, therefore, how these criteria apply to the various programs from which universities try to derive surplus revenue.

Cross-subsidies

Not all university programs that yield a surplus are subject to criticism, or are even open to the charge of being commercially motivated. A lot of innocent cross-subsidization occurs, and must occur, on every campus. The per student costs of different majors and courses of study are bound to vary; concentrators in the sciences, for example, will require more expensive equipment and closer supervision than classics students, while popular majors, such as history and economics, will have economies of scale not available to smaller programs, such as Russian literature. Hence, certain courses of study may result in savings that are used to defray the added expense of others, especially in colleges that are not well endowed. Yet no one expects institutions to charge some students more or less than others to reflect these varying costs. The accounting problems would make such adjustments extremely arbitrary and cumbersome, and students would resent having to pay different amounts for the same degree.

A closer question arises when a university "taxes" its law school or its business school to provide extra resources for its education faculty or divinity school. In such cases, the university is deliberately using its law and management faculties to subsidize other academic programs. Nevertheless, neither of these schools is a likely candidate for exploitation by the central administration. Since both faculties contribute significantly to a university's reputation, the administration cannot afford to risk having them fall behind the competition in obvious ways, nor could it readily do so over the opposition of faculty and alumni. Even a cursory look at most schools of law and business will show that they are much better off than the faculties they are subsidizing and that their salaries and facilities are well above average for the institution. Thus, there is little reason to suspect that the university is improperly jeopardizing the interests of its law and business students and every indication that the surpluses are being used to meet urgent educational needs elsewhere.

Executive Education

Similar considerations help to justify profitable executive programs for corporate officials. Such courses can be highly lucrative, so much so that no one can be entirely sure whether the primary motive for offering them is money or education. On balance, however, the special characteristics of executive education minimize the risk to academic values and ultimately justify the enterprise.

Like patents, executive education serves a useful purpose that is becoming more valuable every year as the tasks American managers face grow increasingly complex. The "customers" for these programs are corporations that know their own needs and are quite capable of protecting their interests. True, one wonders why some leading faculties are able to make such large profits from executive courses, the more so since disagreements persist, even among prominent business school professors, over how much value actually comes from management training.[2] Still, companies are much better equipped than individual students to assess the worth of an executive program. Corporate officials can question former students, observe the effects of the training on the subsequent performance of participants, and make detailed comparisons with a wide array of other programs. If a company finds that a course improves the performance of important executives, the value added easily justifies paying a generous sum to the university. Under these circumstances, far from encouraging exploitation or inferior education, the profit motive attracts more suppliers and intensifies a competition that forces them all to work continuously to improve the quality of their offerings in order to satisfy their customers and retain their business.

This is not to say that profitable programs of corporate executives present no problems. Some well-known business schools have received ample sums from large companies to offer courses of an elementary sort to entry-level executives. Such offerings provide little or no intellectual challenge to the faculty, nor are they given as part of a program created to achieve an important educational goal. Instead, they belong to a growing collection of campus activities of an academic nature, ranging from conferences to executive programs to the routine testing of drugs in which the animating purpose is not to further the intellectual aims of the institution but simply to make money.

Such endeavors carry substantial risks. They distort the priorities of the institution by diverting the energies of scholars and scientists to research and teaching assignments that the university would not undertake were it not for the desire to earn a profit. They often lead campus officials to pressure younger, more vulnerable faculty members into taking on work that they would prefer not to do and that contributes little to their professional development. Because the need for money is never-ending, such activities can easily become addictive, luring the institution into more and more ventures undertaken for financial rather than intellectual reasons. As these initiatives multiply, they are likely to undermine the morale of faculty who prefer to think that academic programs are mounted for genuine intellectual reasons, not simply for pecuniary gain. In view of these dangers, universities may legitimately earn a surplus from executive programs, but they make a mistake if they launch such courses (or any other academic initiatives) with the primary aim of making a profit rather than serving some substantial academic purpose.

Extension Programs

Even more problematic is the practice in many universities of earning a profit from extension courses. Compared with executive training, the competition among providers is less intense, and the "customers" are not business enterprises but working people and housewives, who are typically much less prepared than corporate officials to judge the quality of the courses offered them. Unlike schools of law and business, extension divisions are usually far down the campus hierarchy and have little power to defend their interests from the demands of the university's financial officers. The meager stipends paid to most extension instructors and the frequent lack of any financial aid suggest that sponsoring universities are not offering first-rate programs, but are using them instead to make money to pursue other ends at the expense of the students.

Campus officials will doubtless argue that profits from extension are being directed to more important educational purposes in the college or the graduate school. But is it really clear that profits made from extension courses will be put to better use elsewhere instead of keeping them to improve the continuing education program? Already, colleges and graduate schools have far greater resources than the extension division by virtue of the endowments and gifts provided by generations of loyal alumni. One cannot simply assume that adding still more money to these programs will be more valuable than creating scholarships to help poor students take extension courses that will give them the knowledge and skills to begin a new career.

University officials may reply that they are in the best position to make wise decisions in cases of this sort. Yet one cannot always be sure that the choices these officials make will represent a considered judgment on the academic merits. Presidents and deans do not necessarily allocate funds to achieve the greatest educational results (assuming one could even know what choices such a goal would entail). Often, they act to enhance their institution's visibility and prestige, which may not always be the same thing. Thus, instead of distributing scholarship money to the neediest or most deserving students, they may offer merit scholarships to students who could afford to attend college anyway but whose presence will enhance the academic profile of the entering class. Rather than invest in efforts to improve the quality of teaching, they may upgrade the coaching staff of the football team. Instead of hiring more qualified instructors to teach English composition, they may spend more money luring well-known scholars from other universities at very high salaries, a practice that may enrich the professors and enhance the school's reputation but will seldom do much to improve the quality of higher education as a whole.

It is not surprising that university leaders sometimes make such choices. In the absence of better information, most of them are judged, at least in part, by relatively crude measures that are easy to observe and apply, such as how far SAT scores have risen, whether rankings in *U.S. News and World Report* have improved, and how much money has been raised to start new programs and build new buildings. Like political leaders, their success depends much more on the support of groups that can help them achieve these goals than on weak, dispersed constituencies. As a result, when university officials take money from continuing education and give it to the medical school or the faculty of arts and sciences, they do not necessarily act on purely academic grounds. Rather, their decision may be influenced by the fact that the other faculties are supported by influential professors and alumni and are nationally ranked in publications such as *U.S. News and World Report*, while extension programs are not.

All in all, the use of extension schools as profit centers

seems hard to defend. These schools have fewer resources than almost any other academic unit in the university. Extracting money from them to finance other parts of the institution threatens to compromise a basic academic value by using a potentially worthwhile educational program for purposes other than giving the best instruction possible to its students.

Profiting from the Internet

The Internet offers the most exciting opportunity in years for universities to improve the quality of their education and make it accessible to larger numbers of people. Universities are well situated to capitalize on these possibilities if they choose to do so. But educators follow a treacherous course if they try to use the Internet for profit, especially when they join with venture capitalists to achieve their ends. Even if they retain a controlling interest in the new distance learning organization, their partners will insist on certain rights to protect their investments, such as the right to help choose the top executives or at least to have a veto right over the candidates. It is naive to think that private investors will risk millions of dollars and not use their leverage to insist that the new enterprise conduct its affairs to produce a handsome return.

The dangers involved may be modest if the for-profit ventures confine themselves to executive training programs. Corporate customers are well equipped to know their needs, evaluate the product, and protect themselves from exploitation. But universities are not likely to limit themselves to these customers. Only a few leading institutions with quality programs and the best "brand names" can make large profits in this crowded market; the rest will have to settle for modest returns or drop out of the competition entirely. Thus, many universities will be tempted to move to other hunting grounds with less discerning game: school-teachers trying to upgrade their credentials, recent college graduates seeking to earn a degree in law or business without having to leave their jobs, high school graduates pursuing a college education while continuing to work. Even more inviting is the vast overseas market filled with unsophisticated students hoping to improve their prospects by obtaining a credential from a well-known American university. This possibility has not escaped the notice of venture capitalists. Referring to several prominent for-profit companies started with university participation, two analysts noted that "although these concerns initially targeted the U.S. market, most claimed that the customer base in Asia and South America represented the largest potential market for their services."[3]

For-profit, on-line education aimed at unwary audiences carries a grave risk of exploiting students. The latter are often overly impressed by brand names and at a loss to know which courses will help them most. These conditions favor precisely the wrong kinds of instruction.

The promise of the new educational technology lies in developing highly interactive classes that make good use of simulations, case-method discussions, games, and other means of provoking discussion among students and instructors. But this is the most expensive type of distance education and will probably cost as least as much as conventional campus courses. The way to make big money with the Internet is to attract large audiences with polished lectures by well-known figures, supplemented by attractive visuals and carefully crafted materials, but with a minimum of feedback and interactivity in order to keep down marginal costs and take full advantage of economies of scale. The courses that result may seem attractive, but they will fall far short of achieving the full potential of the new technology.[4] In order to enlarge the size of their audience, providers will favor simpler material over more intellectually demanding coursework. By minimizing interactivity, they will cause their students to learn less. In these ways, the profit motive will lead universities to offer inferior instruction by trading on their reputation and on the gullibility of their students.

There is no compelling reason why universities interested in distance education should have to use a for-profit model and invite venture capitalists to participate. No reputable academic institution has ever created a business school or any other traditional faculty on such a basis. Why should it do so merely because it is using a different medium of instruction?

Internet courses can be expensive, but most universities have substantial assets they could invest in the enterprise, and all of them are proficient in attracting funds from foundations and other private sources. Institutions that have rejected the profit-making model have found that it is possible to recruit the talent required for such an initiative without offering prospective employees a slice of equity. Hence, educators have no compelling need to follow a course so likely to end by compromising academic values. It would be far better, instead, to proceed in a more conventional manner. If universities eventually find that they can offer high-quality Internet courses and still make a profit, they could use the surplus to develop new and creative uses of the Internet throughout the campus instead of diverting the funds to other programs where the intellectual gains are likely to be smaller and considerably less exciting. In this way, universities could utilize their profits to improve the quality of education for everyone in the institution, including those who helped to generate the surplus in the first place.

Commercial Advertising and the Hidden Curriculum

Not all education takes place in classrooms. Intentionally or not, the actions and policies of campus officials carry messages to the university community about which values truly count and which are expendable.[5] At times, these messages can be more powerful than any formal classroom lecture in setting examples that show what the institution truly stands for and what principles really matter.

To illustrate, suppose that the Coca-Cola company approached Princeton University with an offer of $25 million for permission to etch five simple words over the entrance to Nassau Hall: "Things Go Better with Coke." (If this seems far-fetched, consider the company's effort to organize "Coke in Education Day" at high schools, complete with a prize for the best plan for marketing Coke-sponsored discount cards, lectures on economics by Coca-Cola officials, technical assistance to home economics students baking Coca-Cola cakes, not to mention help for chemistry classes analyzing Coca-Cola's sugar content, and even an aerial photograph of the entire student body holding up the letters COKE.)[6]

Princeton would doubtless reject an offer to decorate its entrance in this way. But why? On strict cost-benefit grounds, what are a few harmless words on a building compared with the professorships and scholarships that $25 million would buy? Is it that the inscription would constitute an endorsement of Coca-Cola? Not necessarily. Universities have accepted professorships carrying the name of corporations, even named buildings after a company, without clearly implying institutional approval of the products involved.

The problem goes deeper. To agree to the inscription in a location so emblematic of the university would indicate to everyone on campus that money can buy almost anything at Princeton. No place is too sacred if the price is right. Such a message would be damaging to students and demoralizing for many members of the faculty who believe that their academic careers and the institution where they work stand for aims and ideals that transcend money. By communicating its materialism so brazenly, the university would threaten to undermine any other efforts it makes to keep commercial pressures from eroding academic values.

Similar issues can arise in deciding whether to lend the university's facilities, its athletic uniforms, or simply its name to commercial advertisers in exchange for money. Not all of these cases, however, deserve condemnation. Selling advertising space in football programs and college yearbooks may offend a few members of the university community, but such practices are by now so familiar and seem so innocuous that they do not carry the message of rampant commercialism that makes the inscription on Nassau Hall so objectionable. A far different situation exists when commercial advertisers seek to invade the realm of education. Fortunately, universities have not yet allowed companies to tout their products in campus classrooms. At the periphery of the educational process, however, advertisers wait like predators circling a herd of cattle and occasionally manage to pick off some careless member that strays too far from the group.

The clearest example has occurred in medical schools where large pharmaceutical firms and medical supply companies have become very wealthy at a time when traditional sources of funding for medical education have tended to dry up. These trends have created a vaccuum major corporations are all too willing to fill. By now, corporate representatives commonly recommend speakers paid for at company expense and help shape the content and format of continuing education courses by giving ample subsidies that help medical schools operate their programs at a profit. These practices are clearly worrisome. Although the lecturers subsidized by industrial sponsors may be accomplished faculty members and the quality of the programs is often high, speakers paid for by a pharmaceutical firm and selected from an approved company list cannot be assumed to be as objective and disinterested as university instructors ought to be.* Nor can one be sure that medical faculties will present a completely balanced and unbiased program if companies pay a large portion of the cost and have their representatives act in other subtle ways to influence the proceedings.†[7]

*Some evidence exists that presentations at continuing education programs by speakers funded by pharmaceutical firms do mention the company's products more often and more favorably than competing products. See Marjorie A. Bowman, "The Impact of Drug Company Funding on the Content of Continuing Medical Education," *Mobius* 6 (1986), p. 66.
†A closer case arises when corporate support allows a higher quality of instruction than the medical school could otherwise provide by itself. For example, a surgical supply company may grant a medical school free use of very expensive equipment to teach new surgical techniques to small groups of physicians. The use of the equipment by the school doubtless carries an implicit endorsement and may lead to increased sales. Nevertheless, without the company's help, the school would have to proceed without the equipment and the quality of instruction would suffer. Such situations present a genuine dilemma. Whatever the answer, however, medical schools are unlikely to weigh the competing considerations dispassionately if they treat their continuing education programs as profit centers to support other activities.

To be sure, company-assisted programs are rarely biased in blatant ways to promote the sponsor's product. An audience of practicing physicians would be quick to spot such clumsy marketing efforts, and the program would backfire. Instead, the influence is more subtle and need not even favor one company's product over others. Pharmaceutical companies naturally tend to support programs on diseases commonly treated with expensive drugs. Although the presentations may not tout any particular product, they do promote the use of an entire class of drugs. Moreover, subsidized programs seldom emphasize preventive measures and other alternatives to drug treatments. In these ways, the subsidized programs can be slanted not by what they put in but by what they leave out.

In theory, medical schools can supplement company-sponsored programs with presentations of their own that emphasize prevention and other alternatives to drugs. Nevertheless, given a choice between subsidized programs and programs in which the medical school must pay the full cost, subsidized programs tend to win out. This is particularly likely when schools treat continuing medical education as a profit center to finance other faculty activities.

How serious are the current practices? Doctors taking continuing education courses will deny that the information and the perks they receive from pharmaceutical representatives could ever affect their judgment, just as biomedical researchers routinely deny that their financial interests could possibly influence their treatment of patients in an experiment on human subjects. Such responses seem reassuring, but they are highly suspect. Pharmaceutical companies would hardly spend $2 billion every year sponsoring lectures and other forms of education for physicians if these efforts did not boost sales. Not surprisingly, studies have shown that doctors attending company-sponsored symposia or exposed in other ways to information supplied them by "pharma reps" tend to prescribe the company's products more often.[8] As for the impact of continuing education on the overall use of prescription drugs, no one knows the answer. What *is* clear is that pharmaceutical companies spend very large amounts on continuing medical education and that prescription drugs make up the most rapidly rising component of total health costs in the United States.

The hazards of accepting corporate money and involvement seem sufficiently obvious and serious to warrant stopping such support altogether. The likelihood of bias and the appearance of undue influence are simply too great to be tolerated. Unfortunately, however, decisive action of this sort may no longer be possible. As in big-time football and basketball, medical schools have become so dependent on company subsidies that they will not willingly give them up. The only feasible course, therefore, may be to tighten up the rules to limit the damage. At the very least, medical schools should place a strict ban on any corporate involvement whatsoever in the planning of programs or the content of presentations. Wherever possible, continuing education officials should obtain multiple sponsors to avoid even the appearance of favoring any specific product. Finally, program organizers should recognize a professional obligation monitored by an independent faculty committee to include enough instruction on prevention and other alternatives to drugs that neither individual programs nor the mix of programs carries an implicit bias in favor of prescribing pharmaceutical products.

Drug companies and other corporations may try to associate themselves with the educational offerings of a prominent university even if they have to forgo any influence over the content of the instruction. For example, a major pharmaceutical firm once offered to pay $1 million per year to the Harvard Medical School, along with handsome fees for participating faculty members, to produce a company-sponsored series for cable television on recent developments in cardiology. (This is not an isolated case; one can expect many similar offers if Internet courses begin to attract large audiences.) Under this proposal, Harvard professors would have been solely responsible for developing the information conveyed on the programs, and the company expressly agreed to give the university final authority over all matters of content. Harvard was even allowed to include an express disclaimer during every program making clear that it was not endorsing any of the sponsor's products. But the agreement, of course, did provide for commercial advertising at various points in each episode, thus clearly linking the company and the university in the minds of viewers.

In the end, Harvard chose not to go down that path, concluding that even with these safeguards, it was inappropriate to mix commercial advertising with a university's teaching. The decision was rooted in the importance of having all instruction be (and seem) as objective as possible, motivated only by the desire to communicate knowledge and understanding. Advertising has very different values, animated by an overriding desire to sell the product. Although constrained by law from misrepresenting facts, advertisers continually stretch the truth, engage in hyperbole, omit contrary or qualifying information, and otherwise act in contradiction to standard precepts of good teaching. Since the principles of commercial advertising seemed plainly at odds with the values involved in educating students, mixing the two activities could raise unfortunate questions in the minds of viewers. Accepting paid advertising would clearly indicate to everyone that the university had a pecuniary motive for teaching apart from its desire to educate students. As a result, viewers could justifiably wonder what compromises Harvard might be making in order to earn money and whether its instruction could truly be objective if the truth turned out to conflict with the economic interests of the sponsor.* Since maintaining the audience's trust in the objectivity of the instructor seemed essential to the educational process, the university decided that the risks were ones it ought not take.

Exactly when advertising ceases to be peripheral and begins to impinge upon fundamental educational values is a matter of judgment rather than logic. Stanford bars all advertising in its football stadium, while Georgia Tech accepts $5.5 million from McDonald's to place the golden arches on the floor of its coliseum and on all tickets and game programs. Some institutions do not allow their buildings or their professorships to bear the name of a corporation, while others have no such inhibitions. But no self-respecting university has ever allowed commercial advertising at the beginning and the end of its regular lectures on campus. There is no apparent reason why an institution should abandon this principle merely because its instruction is delivered through a different medium.

---

*One can argue that television news has considerable credibility despite having commercial sponsors. But news programs do things for commercial reasons that no principled university would want to do with its teaching. For example, they have changed the content of their programming in response to their network's desire not to offend powerful sponsors, such as cigarette manufacturers. Moreover, they have altered the content and style of their presentation in questionable ways in an effort to appeal to the largest possible audience. Thus, in the last two decades, local television news has shifted its focus to concentrate more on lurid coverage of crime and personal tragedies.

IMPROVING THE QUALITY OF EDUCATION

The previous discussion has shown how profit-seeking can threaten the university's obligation to give the best possible teaching to its students. Only when competition is keen and the students are well informed about their options and their needs is the profit motive likely to result in first-rate education. Nevertheless, whatever the limitations of for-profit education, it does not follow that the conventional not-for-profit teaching currently supplied by research universities represents the ideal. No responsible observer claims that university faculties pay enough attention to the quality of their instruction or that their educational programs serve the interests of their students as well as they might. By common account, lectures are frequently boring, most of the teaching is too passive, and feedback to students is often too skimpy and too late to be effective.

The discussion, then, seems to have arrived at a discouraging conclusion. Nothing works as well as it should. Neither the profit motive nor the traditional methods of the research university guarantee that faculties will make a serious, sustained effort to improve their methods of instruction and enhance the quality of learning on their campuses. Is this the best we can hope for? Or are there other remedies that could bring about better results than either profit-seeking ventures or conventional university programs seem able to provide?

As an earlier discussion pointed out, a major reason why competition does not yield optimal results in higher education is that students cannot adequately evaluate the options available to them. One way of addressing this problem would be try to improve the methods of constructing the well-known public ratings, such as those in *U.S. News and*

World Report, that help guide student choices and affect institutional behavior. At present, these rankings rely on dubious measures such as average student scores on standardized tests or the opinions of officials in other institutions.* None of these criteria promise any reward to institutions that try to improve the quality of their education. Not surprisingly, therefore, recent studies reveal that *U.S. News and World Report* ratings correlate only weakly or not at all with how extensively colleges use what research has shown to be the most effective methods of teaching and learning.[9]

What could be done to improve matters? Publishing the results of a survey of recent graduates that revealed what they thought about the quality of their education would be a small step in the right direction. An even better move would be to supplement the conventional rankings with an assessment of how much use each institution makes of widely recognized methods of effective teaching and learning, such as greater faculty-student interaction, more writing assignments, or smaller and more participatory classes.[10] Improved in this way, college ratings could give better guidance to educational leaders, faculty, and prospective students, while helping the market work more effectively to cause competing institutions to enhance the quality of their educational programs.

The same is true of programs offered by Internet. If online courses succeed in attracting substantial audiences, competing programs could be evaluated, using the best

*Using SAT scores to rate colleges assumes that colleges offering a higher quality of education attract brighter students, a questionable assumption since students know relatively little about how much they will learn and develop at the various schools they are considering. Using the opinions of college officials assumes that most officials know a good deal about the quality of education at a number of other institutions, which seems highly unlikely.

available measures. Such assessments ought to be more re-liable than college ratings, since trained observers could ex-amine Internet programs directly instead of having to rely on student judgments or other indirect measures. Once again, by giving better information to prospective students, professional evaluations would help market forces bring about higher-quality education and diminish the risk that commercialization will exploit the unwary by offering them appealing but inferior instruction.

Government agencies and foundations could also play a useful role by making more funds available for research and experimentation on ways to improve the effectiveness of teaching, subject to a condition that all programs and ini-tiatives receiving such support be carefully evaluated and the results made publicly known. The Mellon Foundation has already created a model program of this kind to fund experiments with new ways of using technology to reduce costs and increase learning. But money of this kind is still hard to find. The most efficient way to provide it is from a central source, since the costs of carefully organized experi-ments can be substantial for a single campus, while the re-sults will be of use to many other institutions. Carefully ad-ministered, such funding could induce universities to make much greater efforts to investigate new methods of instruc-tion at a time when technological improvements and ad-vances in cognitive science make experiments of this kind especially promising.

Presidents and deans could likewise do a lot to increase the incentives to teach well, even though they have little di-rect control over the way professors conduct themselves in the classroom. In discussing this subject, most critics urge universities to place greater emphasis on teaching in all ap-pointment and promotion proceedings. The point is well taken, but much more than this is needed. Reforming appointments procedures will accomplish little to motivate graduate teaching assistants, who do not expect to remain and be appointed to a faculty position. Nor will it help to sustain the motivation of the senior faculty through all the years after they receive tenure.

An active administration could begin to fill these gaps by doing more to determine how much students have learned during their course of study. To be sure, adequate measures are not available for all subjects, and efforts to use inadequate instruments may trivialize important subjects. Nevertheless, satisfactory methods of assessment seem feasible for a number of subjects, such as writing, mathematics, foreign languages, and analytic reasoning, or even for entire fields of concentration. Properly used, such instruments might help faculties and departments gain a clearer sense of how their students are progressing and where improvements in teaching are especially needed.

Presidents and deans could also require student evaluations of all courses and sections. Despite recurring faculty comment that such assessments are little more than popularity contests, there is a considerable body of research showing that results from carefully constructed student questionnaires correlate reasonably well with independent evaluations by experts.[11] Moreover, thoughtfully crafted evaluations not only provide useful feedback to instructors at all levels; they are also a potent source of motivation, since few members of the faculty wish to see themselves publicly labeled as mediocre teachers in an official campus publication.

In the case of graduate teaching assistants and junior faculty, deans could supplement student evaluations by collecting videotapes of actual classes and other relevant evidence of teaching experience to form a portfolio that these instructors could send to colleges where they applied for jobs. Apart from preparing candidates to present themselves more effectively, such portfolios would demonstrate that good teaching could help secure future employment, which would in turn motivate teaching fellows and young faculty to work harder at improving their classroom skills.

To be fully effective, efforts to strengthen incentives must be accompanied by opportunities for instructors to receive assistance in improving their teaching. Student evaluations provide a first step in this direction by informing teachers about their weaknesses. But there is much more that administrators could do. They could encourage teachers to have their classes videotaped and to watch the results with the aid of an experienced critic. Deans might organize seminars in which graduate students and younger faculty could discuss recurring classroom problems and analyze different responses suggested by successful teachers. To this end, some universities have already made good use of short films to illustrate classroom dilemmas and provoke discussion. Others have had success with microteaching, in which groups of instructors meet and have individual members take turns teaching a brief segment of a class followed by a friendly critique from their colleagues.

In addition to these practical steps, presidents and deans could initiate a process of informed experimentation to discover and disseminate new ways of teaching more effectively. A modest way to begin would be to offer small grants to faculty members who wish to try new methods of instruction with a stipulation that each project be carefully evaluated. A more ambitious program would include a series of experiments with group learning, new uses of the Internet, computer-assisted instruction, and other promising methods. The experiments could either occur in multisection courses, where some sections can serve as control groups, or in subjects such as mathematics, science, and foreign languages, where effects on student learning are more easily measured. The results could then be publicized widely in an effort to encourage other faculty members to make use of the most promising new methods.

Finally, deans and presidents could establish prizes and other forms of recognition that honor good teaching. By themselves, of course, such measures are only gestures that accomplish little. If they are not backed up by other policies of the kind described above, they may even seem hypocritical and evoke cynicism. In conjunction with an array of other initiatives, however, prizes and awards may provide a useful way of reminding faculty and students of the importance the institution attaches to good teaching.

Every university has taken some of these steps, but very few have taken all, or even nearly all, of them. Yet it is the cumulative effect of many separate measures that can change the incentive structure and gradually alter the relative weight given to research and teaching. Priorities on a campus are not immutable. If they seem so, it is often because too little effort has been made to change them. With help from outside funding sources and from those who rank institutions, a determined administration may yet bring the two principal functions of the university into a more fruitful balance without having to rely on the incentives of the commercial marketplace.

10 | LIVING UP TO THE RULES

Setting clear guidelines is essential to protect academic values from excessive commercialization. But guidelines alone, however thoughtfully devised, will not be enough. Cases will inevitably arise in which the rules are ambiguous, the circumstances novel, or the deviations arguably minor. Enterprising aides will think of clever arguments to justify going forward. In such situations, it is neither realistic nor fair to expect that presidents and their deans will consistently summon the resolve to make the proper decisions. The prospect of new revenue is a powerful temptation that can easily lead decent people into unwise compromises, especially when they are under pressure to accomplish more than they can readily achieve by conventional means. Unless the system of governance has safeguards and methods of accountability that encourage university officials to act appropriately, the lure of making money will gradually erode the institution's standards and draw it into more and more questionable practices.

Unfortunately, the structure of governance in most universities is not equal to the challenge of resisting the excesses of commercialization. Presidents and deans are ultimately responsible for upholding basic academic values, but they are exposed to strong conflicting pressures that make it hard for them to carry out this duty effectively.

They are the ones primarily responsible for finding the funds their institutions need to survive and prosper. Balancing the budget is not enough; they must attract outstanding (and expensive) scholars, build new facilities, and improve student services. Continuous competition from other universities and constant requests for new programs from department chairs and other professors create a relentless demand for greater resources. Driven by these financial needs, university leaders rarely encounter any constituent pressures or procedural safeguards strong enough to force them to conduct their search for funds with a consistent respect for academic values.

Trustees are supposed to oversee the work of the president, but it is a rare board that pays close attention to the methods used to attract more funds unless they raise significant legal or public relations problems. Faculty members can be counted upon to stand up for academic freedom and intellectual honesty, but they will usually concern themselves only intermittently with the university's commercial dealings. Students have protested some business ties, such as investments in South Africa or in companies that make extensive use of child labor overseas. Only rarely, however, have they actively opposed the kinds of commercialization explored in this volume.

In short, as the former head of the Association of American Universities once observed, "there is no natural constituency or organized interest group to resist the imposition of bottom-line, short-term considerations."[1] Instead, university presidents and deans are left largely on their own to cope as best they can with the constant demands for added revenue. Their position is too isolated and precarious. If universities are to keep commercialization within reasonable bounds, reinforcements must be found.

TRUSTEES

Trustees could do much more than they typically do to strengthen the university's defenses. They could take pains to establish criteria for evaluating the president that include not only a demonstrated capacity to accomplish goals costing large amounts of money, but also a consistent respect for academic standards even when they conflict with the quest for more resources. They could also insist that the president develop similar criteria for evaluating other university officials in exposed positions on the front lines of commercialization. Athletic directors, continuing education heads, deans of business and medicine, chiefs of technology transfer offices all face recurring tension between attempting to meet financial expectations and upholding proper academic standards. Too often, they are made to feel that the former dominates the latter. Unless they genuinely believe that they will be rewarded for respecting academic values and supported when they resist inappropriate demands, they are unlikely to resist the pressure to make dubious compromises that promise to bring added revenue to their institution.

By exercising proper oversight, trustees could also help ensure a consistent respect for academic principles throughout the university. They could ask for annual reports on the academic qualifications of entering student-athletes, especially in the revenue-producing sports, along with statistics on the graduation rates of all those receiving athletic scholarships. They could review university rules on conflicts of interest, evaluate limits on the secrecy allowed to corporate research sponsors, and examine the procedures for ensuring compliance. They could ask to be informed of all for-profit educational programs and approve them only after assuring themselves that adequate procedures and faculty oversight exist to guarantee proper levels of quality. Finally, they could conduct regular audits to determine whether all rules and procedures that protect academic values are actually being observed in practice.

Although vigilant boards could do a lot to ensure a decent respect for academic values, one cannot count on them to do the whole job themselves. Indeed, the sad fact is that in dealing with the commercialization of athletics over many years, trustees have more often been part of the problem than part of the solution.[2] Their performance is unlikely to improve significantly so long as current methods for selecting board members remain the same. At many state universities, the governors who choose trustees make most of their appointments to satisfy particular constituencies or to repay political supporters. Such boards rarely include many members who are qualified to help their institutions meet the kinds of challenges outlined in these pages.[3] Private universities usually do a better job of choosing trustees, but even they are generally inclined to place heavy emphasis on appointing individuals whose principal qualification is a capacity to contribute financially.

Even the most distinguished boards will typically have few, if any, members who know universities well enough to have an instinctive sense of how revenue-seeking initiatives can threaten intellectual standards. Moreover, in the best of circumstances, trustees have only limited time and many other duties to perform. Meeting only occasionally, they cannot keep close enough watch on campus life to detect the slow erosion of academic values. For that, one must enlist the help of other members of the university community.

THE FACULTY

Of all the major constituencies in a university, faculty members are in the best position to appreciate academic values and insist on their observance. Since they work on campus, they are better situated than trustees to observe what is going on. They have the most experience with academic programs and how they work. Most of all, they have the greatest stake in preserving proper academic standards and principles, since these values protect the integrity of their work and help perpetuate its quality.

Proper faculty oversight will not come automatically. Professors are busy people, too preoccupied with their own classes, their own departments, and their own research to see the campus whole or appreciate its larger problems and opportunities. Content with what is surely one of the freest, most absorbing vocations in America and consumed by the multiple opportunities and demands of academic life, they are normally inclined to stay aloof from the larger affairs of the institution and to resist administrative initiatives that threaten to make new demands on their time. While they have a personal interest in paying close attention to appointments and other issues affecting their own department, most problems involving the university as a whole seem too remote to tempt them to get involved.

How can university governance take greater advantage of the best qualities of faculty and administration while guarding against their weaknesses? How can it combine the desire of energetic university leaders to innovate and adapt to new pressures and opportunities with the faculty's sensitivity to the importance of preserving basic academic values? Solving this problem creatively and well represents the principal challenge to the modern university in trying to

benefit from the opportunities of the commercial marketplace without losing its integrity in the process.

At present, universities are having a hard time meeting
this challenge. Most of them have some form of faculty
governance in which professors participate with the administration in crafting academic policy. Without constant attention and encouragement, however, such systems can
quickly fall into disrepair. Many governing bodies that include members of the faculty are populated by professors of
lesser distinction who debate at great length without com-
manding much respect from their colleagues. Many more
are too large to deal expeditiously with the problems before
them. The participants are not accountable for their performance, nor do they receive any reward if they perform
well. Some are selected for the wrong reasons. For example,
athletics committees often include faculty members who
volunteer because they are more rabid about college sports
than the athletic director himself. Committees of all kinds
typically include women, minorities, and representatives
of other prominent constituencies whether or not these
members have any special competence to deal with the issues of commercialization. As a result, committees often
have too few professors possessing relevant knowledge and
experience and too many who are appointed for other reasons. Under these conditions, faculty governance can easily
sink into longer and longer debates about less and less, ac-
complishing little of real importance for professors while
causing frustration and delay for the administration.

The danger, then, is that universities will be burdened
with a system of governance that combines the worst rather
than the best features of the administration and faculty.
Around the periphery of the institution, presidents and
deans will unilaterally launch questionable schemes of dis-

tance learning and commercial research, while at the heart of the university, professors passively resist efforts to innovate and experiment with new methods of instruction to improve the quality of education.

This unfortunate state of affairs already exists on a number of campuses. Impatient at the thought of being mired in endless debate, enterprising presidents and deans are increasingly tempted to bypass faculty review when launching new entrepreneurial ventures. Detailed accounts of commercialization, both here and abroad, repeatedly document this tendency. In their thoughtful study of the "enterprise university" in Australia, Simon Marginson and Mark Considine observed that "without exception the university leaders in our study saw collegial forms of decision-making as an obstacle to managerial rationalities"[5] The same trend seems to be occurring in the United States, as well. In one faculty survey, 73 percent of respondents from U.S. universities reported that "decision-making had become more bureaucratic, top-down, centralized, automatic, and managerial."[5] At Columbia University, Dean Feldberg's decision to have his Business School collaborate with the Internet education company (U.Next) was taken without any discussion with his faculty. "I made the decision," Feldberg said. "I didn't take it to the faculty." "I saw the opportunity to participate in the market value of this company and to increase the endowment of the school," he added, noting with concern that Columbia's business school had an endowment barely one-eighth the size of Harvard's.[6]

Unilateral decisions of this kind are an invitation to trouble. Innovative breakthroughs in teaching and research, such as creative applications of Internet technology, will rarely come from top-down management. They are much more likely to emerge from experiments by imaginative faculty members or from collaborative groups of professors operating with the support of the administration but not under its control. Thus, as Marginson and Considine point out, "Reinvention [i.e., entrepreneurial] strategies not underpinned by academic strength face severe limits. . . . In the medium term, management, marketing, and reinvention are sometimes enough. In the long term, reliance on management as *the* driver tends to choke off academic development. . . . If reinvention worked *through* academic cultures, actively engaging them, a larger, more exciting and more educationally enriching range of reinventions might become possible."[7] Not to mention a greater likelihood of avoiding embarrassing commercial misadventures.

There is much talk today of the need for quick, streamlined mechanisms for making decisions to exploit new opportunities in a rapidly changing world. Shared governance and faculty participation, it is said, are expensive luxuries that enterprising universities can no longer afford if they wish to keep up with the competition. Such statements may sound plausible, but there is actually very little evidence to support them. In the history of commercializing higher education, one can much more easily find hasty, misguided profit-seeking ventures than point to truly valuable opportunities that were lost through prolonged faculty debate.

This is not to say that university officials must necessarily work within the existing structures of faculty governance and put up with all of its frustrations. New procedures and new entities may be called for to fit the special circumstances of new entrepreneurial ventures. For certain kinds of problems, smaller faculty groups may be required, composed of members whose experience equips them to understand the issues and the values involved.

Still, the central point remains that universities will do a better job of upholding essential values if faculty members help design and oversee all profit-making or commercial activities that affect the academic life of the university: the athletics department, the continuing education division, the executive programs, and the patent licensing and technology transfer offices.

However they organize their committees and other consultative bodies, university leaders will certainly need to secure the participation of highly respected professors. Even if there are no conventional rewards for conscientious performance, faculty members can be motivated if the issues seem interesting and significant, and they can feel that they are making a contribution. Thus, it is essential to involve them in meaningful discussions about the important policies and programs of the institution and to give enough weight to what they say to convince them that they can have a real influence on policy. Throughout, the aim should be to build a system of governance that uses the strengths of both the faculty and administration by educating the former about the larger needs and opportunities of the university while keeping the latter attentive to the essential values and standards that are required to maintain the highest attainable intellectual quality.

HANGING TOGETHER

Agreements with other universities offer a third line of defense against excessive commercialization. Competition among institutions often provides a valuable stimulus, but it can also create a powerful force to erode academic principles. No university can insist for very long on appropriate conflict-of-interest rules and watch distinguished professors move to other universities that are content to have lax procedures. Nor can any institution uphold reasonable admissions standards and have its football team humiliated week after week by less scrupulous opponents. Agreements with competing institutions, therefore, offer an essential way to neutralize destructive competitive pressures.

In the Ivy League, for example, members have committed themselves not to give athletic scholarships, not to admit athletes with prior grades and test scores substantially below the levels of their classmates, and not to schedule mid-week games that force students to miss classes. No member school could abide by such rules without the agreement of the others. In similar fashion, major research universities could agree on uniform rules governing the sharing of research materials, or conflicts of interest in clinical research, or appropriate limits on the degree of secrecy allowable in research contracts with corporations. Leading medical journals have already adopted a similar strategy by agreeing not to accept articles reporting company-sponsored clinical research without satisfactory assurances that no undue influence was exerted by the sponsors over the results. Medical schools would do well to follow this example by pledging not to accept any corporate funding for clinical research without satisfactory guarantees to ensure that investigators retain full control over the experiments and are free to publish all of the results.*

---

*Of course, university compacts of this kind could be used in questionable ways to limit the royalties and other legitimate outside earnings of professors. There are antitrust laws, however, to prevent improper arrangements of this kind. Within legal limits, well-crafted agreements can play an indispensable role in enabling universities to resist undue commercialization.

THE ROLE OF GOVERNMENT

Although voluntary agreements among universities can be extremely helpful, they are usually hard to negotiate, even within a single athletic conference or academic group. Member schools are often different enough from one another that it is difficult to arrive at rules suitable to all. For example, the Pac-10 and Big-10 conferences will have a hard time agreeing on common admissions standards, since both leagues include private institutions with highly selective student bodies and much larger public universities with far lower entrance requirements. Moreover, university presidents may not all acknowledge the need for an agreement or accept the proposed terms, either because they have sharply differing financial situations or simply because they have conflicting views about what needs to be done.

Because of these difficulties, it is tempting to look toward Washington for solutions. Governments can impose limits, even if universities are unable to agree among themselves. Legislators are motivated, at least in theory, by the public interest rather than the self-serving concerns of universities. Once the government acts, moreover, its decrees do not rely on voluntary compliance but are enforced by the full authority of the state.

Notwithstanding these advantages, relying on government to solve the problems of commercialization would be a mistake. If it is hard for presidents to agree on common solutions for heterogeneous institutions, it is even harder for legislators to devise enlightened, workable rules, unfamiliar as they are with all of the special problems and conditions of research universities. In practice, moreover, the legislative process is a messy affair, subject to hasty, last minute compromises and quiet concessions to special interests. The outcome of this process is often less than ideal. Even Title IX—though beneficial overall for women athletes—gives an excessively simple solution to a complex set of problems. In college sports as a whole, far from offering a cure for the woes of big-time athletics, legislators in many states are a major reason why genuine reform is not possible. Similarly, in their zeal to further economic growth through campus-corporate cooperation, lawmakers might do more to undermine academic values than to preserve them.

These limitations hardly justify immunity from government regulation; the state must intervene to protect legitimate interests apart from the universities themselves. Thus, lawmakers have to decide such issues as when profits from commercial activities represent unrelated income for tax purposes, or how to define the proper scope of patentability, or what restrictions are needed to protect human subjects in medical research. The threat of such legislation can even be a useful spur to prod university leaders to accept appropriate private agreements in order to avoid government intervention. But neither Congress nor the legislatures in the individual states would be well advised to assume the task of protecting academic values by imposing limits to commercialization. The risk is simply too great that the government's remedies will end by doing more harm than good.

Public officials should also be aware of the influence of government funding on the growth of commercialization. The last line of defense for basic academic standards is an adequate and stable level of support. As a practical matter, survival will almost always take precedence over institutional values. Already, the loss of public funds for advanced medical training has caused many teaching hospitals to allow pharmaceutical representatives into their buildings to provide free lunches where they lecture to interns and residents and openly promote their products. Severe financial pressures have brought about even greater commercialization in many public schools, ranging from taking money in return for exclusive contracts to sell unhealthy soft drinks and packaged foods in school vending machines to using "free" school materials that combine commercial advertising with math and science instruction. Across the nation, students today are studying chemistry by showing that Prego spaghetti sauce is truly thicker than its leading competitors, or learning mathematics by trying to prove how many chocolate chips there are in every bag of Chips Ahoy cookies.[8]

In much the same way, if federal support for science is cut severely, the balance will shift too far from basic inquiry toward applied, commercially funded research. If public universities find their state budget allocations sharply reduced over a sustained period, they will surely try to extract more profit from extension divisions and distance learning programs, even at a sacrifice in educational quality. Fortunately, government support for higher education in the United States has tended to be generous in the past; that is an important reason for the excellent reputation American universities enjoy around the world. Hence, the intent here is not to register a complaint but simply to make clear that reasonable financial stability is the ultimate guarantee against irresponsible entrepreneurial behavior.

Others may think of further steps to help university leaders resist the excesses of commercialization. Whatever the precise reforms, however, the basic point remains: success demands much more than simply announcing an appropriate set of rules. Unless universities create an environment in which the prevailing incentives and procedures reinforce intellectual standards instead of weakening them, commercial temptations are bound to take a continuing toll on essential academic values.

11 | SEIZING THE MOMENT

Today, American universities face exceptional opportunities and exceptional risks. Their research is needed more than ever now that new discoveries and expert knowledge have become so essential to progress in health care, economic growth, and other endeavors that matter to the nation. As careers grow more complicated and subject to sudden change, adults in all occupations and stages of life are seeking further education at the very moment when technology gives people everywhere ready access to university instruction.

Now that scientific discovery and continuing education are valued so highly, pressures have arisen from every quarter to have universities make their services available to those who need them. State officials ask campuses to speed innovation, job creation, and economic growth by cooperating more closely with industry. Businesses urge universities to do more to train their executives and collaborate scientifically in ways that will lead to valuable new products. Citizens everywhere look for courses of study that will help them qualify for better jobs and promising careers.

These growing demands allow universities and their faculties to profit from academic work in more ways than ever before. Ironically, however, the very same opportunities could easily end by harming the academic enterprise and sullying its contributions to the nation's welfare. As the Har- **199** vard president in the Preface came to realize, making money in the world of commerce often comes with a Faustian bargain in which universities have to compromise their basic values—and thereby risk their very souls—in order to enjoy the rewards of the marketplace.

Although the dangers are real, not all ties with industry are suspect, nor should universities refuse every opportunity to earn a financial return from their work. The money campuses can make from patenting scientific discoveries has elicited much valuable effort to put laboratory advances to practical use. The profits earned from executive training programs have led faculties to work harder to serve legitimate needs. Acting prudently, universities can do a lot to share their knowledge with industry, meet the growing demand for continuing education, and even make some money along the way without damaging themselves in the process.

Thus far, however, university leaders have paid too little heed to the risks that profit-making activities often bring in their wake. Instead, they have eagerly embraced one commercial venture after another in the hope of gaining added revenue for their institution. The end to which this process could lead is not a pleasant prospect to behold. One can imagine a university of the future tenuring professors because they bring in large amounts of patent royalties and industrial funding; paying high salaries to recruit "celebrity" scholars who can attract favorable media coverage; admitting less than fully qualified students in return for handsome parental gifts; soliciting corporate advertising to underwrite popular executive programs; promoting Internet courses of inferior quality while canceling worthy conventional offerings because they cannot cover their costs; encouraging professors to spend more time delivering routine

research services to attract corporate clients, while providing a variety of symposia and "academic" conferences
planned by marketing experts in their development offices
to lure potential donors to the campus. If this vision comes
to pass, university officials will doubtless defend their practices as a means of financing valuable academic pursuits
that cannot pay their way. Yet in the end, one suspects, after
the university finishes paying for unexpectedly high marketing costs, sharing the profits with insistent faculty participants, and absorbing the losses from various failed initiatives, little money will remain to give to other worthwhile
programs.

This picture may seem exaggerated, but it does not go
very far beyond existing practices. There is not much difference between granting admission in return for a handsome
gift and giving preference to the children of major donors.
Nor is a growing corporate influence over curricula more
than an extension of current methods of organizing continuing education programs for doctors. Universities may not
yet be willing to trade all of their academic values for
money, but they have proceeded much further down that
road than they are generally willing to acknowledge.

For example, to sustain their athletic programs, most colleges currently admit from 5 percent of all their students (in
public universities) to more than 30 percent (in liberal arts
colleges) with the expectation that they will play on varsity
teams.[1] While some of these students would be welcome
even if they had no athletic ability, many would never be
admitted save for a talent that bears no necessary relation to
the true mission of the university.

For high-profile, revenue-producing sports, such as football and basketball, the compromises with academic standards are particularly severe. In most of these programs,

education is completely subordinate to the demands of the sport. Most of the athletes involved enter with academic credentials far below those of their classmates. Once admitted, they either fail to graduate or finish only with the help of intensive tutoring, frequently taking courses of questionable rigor specially designed for them.

Unfortunately, the effects of intercollegiate athletics are by no means confined to a few major sports or to a select group of schools that maintain big-time programs. Even small liberal arts colleges assemble football, basketball, and hockey teams by admitting students recruited by their coaching staff with test scores substantially below the school-wide average. More than two-thirds of these students finish in the bottom third of their graduating class. Although such schools do not give athletic scholarships or indulge in many of the worst practices of the big-time universities, their small size leads them to admit much larger proportions (up to one-third) of their entire student body for athletic reasons. As a result, the effects of their athletic recruiting and admissions practices are much more widely felt throughout the college.

Commercialization has also taken a toll on the quality of education. Many institutions, seeking to profit from their correspondence schools and extension divisions, have followed academic policies of a kind they would never allow in their regular degree programs. They have granted little or no financial aid, while keeping faculty compensation well below the normal scale for the rest of the university. As a result, access to these programs has suffered, along with the quality of instruction. In medical schools, pharmaceutical companies offering financial support threaten the objectivity and balance of the programs offered to practicing physicians. In the future, further harm could result from commercializing Internet programs if universities, in their zeal to make money, offer courses that do not take full advantage of the power new technology gives to improve teaching and learning.

The inroads of commercialization on educational values are particularly unfortunate, because they depend, at bottom, on a willingness to take unfair advantage of students. Years ago, correspondence schools resorted to high-pressure marketing coupled with policies that denied students refunds when they tried to drop courses that proved to be disappointing. Today, colleges in Division I arguably exploit their football and basketball players by agreeing with other institutions to restrict their compensation while working them long hours and giving them an education that often falls far short of what other undergraduates receive. Tomorrow, universities may use the Internet to give courses of doubtful quality to unwary individuals eager to gain a credential from a well-known institution. Even if such practices break no laws, it is unworthy of universities to earn money by exploiting students no matter how lofty the purposes for which the profits will allegedly be used. Every action of this kind violates the obligation to make all educational decisions for the benefit of those being taught and not for some ulterior purpose.

In the case of scientific research, the worst fears about the effects of corporate funding have not yet come to pass. Even so, universities have clearly made compromises with standards of behavior long considered important to a healthy process of inquiry. Secrecy has increased and often lasts longer than corporate sponsors need to protect their legitimate interests. Medical faculties have failed to take strong enough measures to prevent conflicts of interest despite evidence that financial considerations can skew the results of clinical research. Universities and their hospitals have not always shielded their faculty from corporate pressure to suppress unfavorable results and have allowed companies to block publication, edit the results, or even write drafts of articles and reports that later appear under the names of faculty investigators. It is impossible to measure the harm that results from these failings. What *is* clear is that most of the damage could have been avoided with little, if any, sacrifice of corporate funding had universities merely been more vigilant in guarding their basic academic values.

Fortunately, researchers have been surprisingly resistant to the worst temptations of commercialism. Contrary to much popular opinion, relatively few scientists chase after lucrative business opportunities at the expense of their teaching duties or research agendas. By most accounts, the time spent consulting outside the university has not increased in recent decades, and professors who consult a lot, teach as much and perform as many administrative chores as their colleagues. By and large, therefore, academic norms have proved to be stronger than the lure of making money.

University leaders would make a great mistake, however, if they assumed that this state of affairs will continue indefinitely. The world of academic science is still dominated by senior figures who grew up and acquired their values in a much less commercial environment. No one knows what will happen when the mantle of authority passes to a generation of researchers who have spent their entire professional lives surrounded by tempting opportunities to start new firms or to help private companies develop lucrative products. There *is* evidence that entrepreneurial activity is most likely to grow in departments that already have a cluster of members engaged in these pursuits.[2] Such findings suggest that if new values begin to take hold and alter the priorities of university scientists, the trend will be increasingly difficult to stop.

These dangers caution against efforts to take technology transfer activities into account in appointing and promoting faculty members. The case for doing so seems persuasive at first glance; if lawmakers and taxpayers expect universities to make a real effort to share their scientific advances with industry, professors who further this effort by seeking patents, starting businesses, and consulting widely should be rewarded by their institutions. Conceivably, such recognition might be justified in the case of professors who are unlikely to make as great a contribution through their own research as they can by sharing existing scientific knowledge with companies. For basic science departments in major universities, however, rewarding professors for technology transfer would be most unwise. The market already rewards such activities. To go further and give credit in appointments proceedings could easily tilt the balance too far toward encouraging commercial pursuits. Universities, in their eagerness to make money, might use such policies to tenure professors of modest scientific talents who demonstrate a capacity to raise substantial funds from patents or industrial connections. In the end, the fragile set of values so critical to basic research could gradually succumb to commercial temptations to the detriment of basic scientific progress.

Although universities show signs of excessive commercialization in every aspect of their work, the trend is not yet irreversible in any area (barring a few high-profile competitive sports). In the all-important domains of education and research, academic leaders still have the power to develop appropriate policies.* But universities are approaching a critical juncture. They can try hard to create and enforce more effective limits on commercialization. Or, they can temporize, compromise, rationalize, and continue the gradual slide into habits that could alter their character in ways detrimental to their teaching, research, and standing in the community.

Why should university leaders want to seize this moment to stop such decay? Setting proper limits and providing supportive structures to maintain them will take a lot of work by faculty, administration, and trustees. Entrepreneurial professors may resist new rules. Boosters may protest athletic reforms. Corporations may occasionally refuse to sign a lucrative research contract. Even so, while the difficulties are real, the cost of continued neglect promises to be even greater. The purely pragmatic university, intent upon increasing its financial resources by any lawful means, may gain a temporary advantage now and then, but it is not an institution that is likely to prosper in the long run.

By compromising basic academic principles, universities tamper with ideals that give meaning to the scholarly community and win respect from the public. These common values are the glue that binds together an institution already fragmented by a host of separate disciplines, research centers, teaching programs, and personal ambitions. They keep the faculty focused on the work of discovery, scholarship, and learning despite the manifold temptations of the outside world. They help maintain high standards of student admissions and faculty appointments. They sustain the belief of scientists and scholars in the worth of what they are

*A possible exception is continuing medical education, where the dependence on corporate support has reached such a point that it will be difficult for medical schools to free themselves of industry influence.

doing. They make academic careers a calling rather than just another way to earn a living.

Defending these academic values, even at the risk of financial sacrifice, evokes the admiration of students, faculty, and alumni, while building the public's trust in what professors say and do. In contrast, when campus authorities let values erode, their moral authority shrinks. Faculty members become less mindful of their responsibilities, less collegial in their relationships, less inclined to take on tasks beyond the minimum required. Individual professors are emboldened to pursue private ventures at a cost to the common enterprise. Inequities and inequalities grow more pronounced, and weaker groups feel impelled to organize collectively to protect themselves. As internal norms give way, formal rules are required to ensure that the work of the institution gets done. If the university will not act, out of fear of offending the faculty, the government will eventually intervene to protect legitimate interests. Bit by bit, therefore, commercialization threatens to change the character of the university in ways that limit its freedom, sap its effectiveness, and lower its standing in the society.

Hard pressed for resources to meet internal demands for quality and growth, universities are understandably tempted to ignore these hazards and take the expedient course. At the outset, the profits to be made seem all too tangible, while the risks appear to be manageable and slight. Most moneymaking ventures start, not with flagrant violations of principle, but with modest compromises that carry few immediate costs. The problems come so gradually and silently that their link to commercialization may not even be perceived. Like individuals who experiment with drugs, therefore, campus officials may believe that they can proceed without serious risk.

Before moving further down this path, university leaders should recall the history of intercollegiate athletics and ponder the lessons it teaches. Confounding expectations, the hoped-for profits often fail to materialize, while the damage to academic standards and institutional integrity proves to be all too real. By this time, unfortunately, the process may be irreversible. Once compromises have been tolerated long enough, universities will find it difficult to re-build the public's trust, regain the faculty's respect, and re-turn to the happier conditions of earlier times. In exchange for ephemeral gains in the continuing struggle for progress and prestige, they will have sacrificed essential values that are all but impossible to restore.

NOTES

CHAPTER ONE THE ROOTS OF COMMERCIALIZATION

1. "The University Presidency," *Atlantic Monthly* 97 (1906), p. 36.

2. *The Higher Learning in America: A Memorandum on the Conduct of Universities by Businessmen* (reprint ed., 1957), p. 209.

3. For a critical account of these developments, see, for example, Robert Kuttner, *Everything for Sale: The Virtues and Limits of Markets* (1996).

4. See Allen Bloom, *The Closing of the American Mind: How Higher Education Has Failed Democracy and Impoverished the Souls of Today's Students* (1987); Bill Readings, *The University in Ruins* (1996); Stanley Aronowitz, *The Knowledge Factory: Dismantling the Corporate University and Creating the Higher Learning* (2000). (Mr. Aronowitz is a sociologist.) This is not a new complaint; the same charge was made around 1900. See Laurence R. Veysey, *The Emergence of the Modern University* (1965), p. 346.

5. See, for example, Wesley Shumar, *College for Sale: A Critique of the Commodification of Higher Education* (1997). For a history of the evolution of boards of trustees and one author's view of its significance, see Clyde W. Barrow, *Universities and the Capitalist State: Corporate Liberalism and the Reconstruction of American Higher Education, 1894–1928* (1990).

6. See Sheila Slaughter and Larry L. Leslie, *Academic Capitalism: Politics, Policies and the Entrepreneurial University* (1997).

7. Ibid. describes the process in Australia.

8. See, for example, Richard Florida, "The Role of the University: Leveraging Talent, not Technology," *Issues in Science and Technology* 15 (1999), p. 67; Raymond Smilor, Glenn B. Dietrich, and David V. Gibson, "The Entrepreneurial University: The Role of Higher Education in the United States in Commer-

cialization and Economic Development," *International Social Studies Journal* (UNESCO) (1993), p. 1.

9. Wesley M. Cohen, Richard Florida, Lucien Randazzese, and John Walsh, "Industry and the Academy: Uneasy Partners in the Cause of Technological Advance," in Roger G. Noll, ed., *Challenges to Research Universities* (1998), pp. 171, 172–82.

10. See, for example, Burton Clark, *Creating Entrepreneurial Universities: Organizational Pathways of Transition* (1998).

11. Stanley Aronowitz, *The Knowledge Factory*, p. 164.

12. Wesley Shumar, *College for Sale*, p. 5.

CHAPTER TWO AVOIDING BIAS

1. Thorstein Veblen, *The Higher Learning in America: A Memorandum on the Conduct of Universities by Businessmen* (1957), p. 139.

2. Abraham Flexner, *Universities, American, English, German* (1930), pp. 152–61. "Modern business does not satisfy the criteria of a profession; it is shrewd, energetic, and clever, rather than intellectual in character; it aims—and under our present social organization must aim—at its own advantage rather than at noble purpose within itself" (p. 154).

3. John Jay Chapman, "The Harvard Classics and Harvard," *Science* 30 (1909), p. 440.

4. Peter Caws "Design for a University," *Daedalus* (Winter 1970), p. 98.

5. Stanley Aronowitz, *The Knowledge Factory: Dismantling the Corporate University and Creating the Higher Learning* (2000), p. 164.

6. Arie P. De Geus, *The Living Company* (1997).

7. Uri Treisman, "Studying Students Studying Calculus: A Look at the Lives of Minority Mathematics Students in College," *The College Mathematics Journal* (1992): 362.

8. See, for example, Kenneth H. Ashworth, "The Texas Case Study," *Change* (Nov.–Dec. 1994), p. 10; and more generally,

Alexander Astin, *Assessment for Excellence: The Philosophy and Practice of Assessment and Evaluation in Higher Education* (1993), p. 216.

CHAPTER THREE ATHLETICS

1. Ronald A. Smith, *Sports and Freedom: The Rise of Big-Time College Athletics* (1988).

2. Edward S. Jordan, "Buying Football Victories," *Colliers* (Nov. 18, 1905), pp. 19–20.

3. Howard J. Savage, *American College Athletics* (1929), p. 28.

4. Donald Chu, Jeffrey Segrave, and Beverly J. Becker, eds., *Sport and Higher Education* (1985), p. 7.

5. Ronald A. Smith, *Sports and Freedom*, p. 84.

6. Ibid., p. 206

7. Henry Pritchett, "Progress of the State Universities," *Carnegie Foundation for the Advancement of Teaching, Annual Report VI* (1911), p. 108.

8. Knight Foundation Commission on Intercollegiate Athletics, *Reconnecting College Sports and Higher Education* (June 2001), p. 18.

9. Quoted in Murray Sperber, *Beer and Circus: How Big-Time Sports Is Crippling Undergraduate Education* (2000), p. 228.

10. Murray Sperber, *College Sports, Inc.: The Athletics Department vs. the University* (1990).

11. Walter Byers, *Unsportsmanlike Conduct: Exploiting College Athletes* (1995), p. 340.

12. James L. Shulman and William G. Bowen, *The Game of Life: College Sports and Educational Values* (2001), p. 257 (hereafter cited as Shulman and Bowen).

13. Quoted by Andrew Zimbalist, *Unpaid Professionals: Commercialization and Conflict in Big-Time College Sports* (1999), p. 29.

14. Knight Foundation Commission, *Reconnecting College Sports*, p. 9.

15. Andrew Zimbalist, *Unpaid Professionals*, p. 25.

16. Walter Byers, *Unsportsmanlike Conduct*, p. 337.

17. Shulman and Bowen, p. 45.

18. Ibid., p. 49.

19. Ibid., p. 48

20. Ibid., p. 62. As Shulman and Bowen point out, it is extremely difficult to obtain an accurate picture of the revenues and costs of athletic programs.

21. Ibid.

22. Ibid., p. 66.

23. Knight Foundation Commission, *Reconnecting College Sports*, p. 15.

24. For a comprehensive study documenting the problems athletes face in being serious students, see the report commissioned in the late 1980s by the President's Committee of the NCAA: *Report No. 1: Summary Results from the 1987–1988 Study of Intercollegiate Athletics* (1988).

25. Murray Sperber, *Beer and Circus*, p. 30.

26. Andrew Zimbalist, *Unpaid Professionals*, p. 39.

27. Quoted in Richard G. Sheehan, *Keeping Score: The Economics of Big-Time Sports* (1996), p. 286.

28. Patricia A. Adler and Peter Adler, *Backboards and Blackboards* (1991), p. 85.

29. Quoted by Shulman and Bowen, p. 78.

30. Adam Smith, *An Inquiry into the Nature and Causes of the Wealth of Nations* (reprint ed., 1939), p. 106.

31. Walter Byers, *Unsportsmanlike Conduct*, p. 369.

32. Quoted in Knight Foundation Commission, *Reconnecting College Sports*, p. 8.

33. Ronald A. Smith, *Sports and Freedom*, p. 171.

34. Quoted in Andrew Zimbalist, *Unpaid Professionals*, p. 3.

35. Ronald A. Smith, *Sports and Freedom*, p. 129.

36. Quoted in Walter Byers, *Unsportsmanlike Conduct*, p. 41.

37. See Shulman and Bowen, pp. 47–49.

38. The research is discussed by Sharon K. Stoll and Jennifer

M. Beller in "Do Sports Build Character?," in John R. Gerdy, ed., *Sports in School: The Future of an Institution* (2000), p. 18.

39. Andrew Zimbalist, *Unpaid Professionals*, p. 176.

40. Ibid.

41. "Study Casts Doubt on Idea that Winning Teams Yield More Applicants," *Chronicle of Higher Education* (March 30, 2001), p. A51.

42. William G. Bowen and Derek Bok, *The Shape of the River: Long-Term Consequences of Considering Race in College and University Admissions* (1998), Appendix Table D.8.4, p. 444.

43. Howard T. Savage, *American College Athletics* (1929), pp. 307–8.

44. Ernest Boyer, *College: The Undergraduate Experience in America* (1987), p. 184.

45. Andrew Zimbalist, *Unpaid Professionals*, pp. 165–67.

46. Shulman and Bowen, p. 221.

47. Sarah E. Turner, Lauren A. Meserve, and William G. Bowen, "Winning and Giving: Football Results and Alumni Giving at Selective Private Colleges and Universities," *Social Science Quarterly* 82 (2001), p. 812. The only category of schools showing a positive relationship between winning and giving was Division III, where athletics are emphasized much less and athletes do not receive athletic scholarships.

48. Shulman and Bowen, pp. 218–19; William G. Bowen and Derek Bok, *The Shape of the River*, pp. 242–46.

49. Shulman and Bowen, p. 223.

50. Ariel Sabar, "Terrapins Image Takes Flight," *Baltimore Sun* (Dec. 31, 2001), p. 1A.

51. James J. Duderstadt, *Intercollegiate Athletics and the American University: A University President's Perspective* (2001), p. 146.

52. As a former president of the University of Michigan put it, "Since, in the general scheme of university priorities, intercollegiate athletics today has such a low relevance to the rest of university life, and its problems seem so intractable, few presidents choose to fight a battle where the personal risks are so large and

the chances of success seem so remote." James J. Duderstadt, *Intercollegiate Athletics and the American University*, p. 304.

53. Jodi Wilgoren, "Spiraling Sports Budgets Draw Fire from Faculties," *New York Times* (July 29, 2001).

54. Frederick Rudolph, *The American College and University: A History* (1962), pp. 373–74.

55. Quoted in Andrew Zimbalist, *Unpaid Professionals*, pp. 92, 227.

56. Ibid., p. 92.

57. The history of NCAA policies toward athletic scholarships is recounted in Allen L. Sack and Ellen S. Stanrowsky, *College Athletes for Hire: The Evolution and Legacy of the NCAA's Amateur Myth* (1988).

58. Howard T. Savage, *American College Athletics*, p. 265.

CHAPTER FOUR SCIENTIFIC RESEARCH

1. John Le Carré, *The Constant Gardener* (2001).

2. Ibid., p. 491.

3. Quoted in Martin Kenney, *Biotechnology: The University-Industrial Complex* (1986), p. 130.

4. Vannevar Bush, *Science: The Endless Frontier* (1945), *http://www1.umn.edu/scitech/assign/vb/V.Bush1945.html.*, p. 16.

5. Martin Kenney, *Biotechnology: The University-Industrial Complex* p. 246.

6. David C. Mowery, Richard R. Nelson, Bhaven N. Sampat, and Arvids A. Ziedonis, "The Effects of the Bayh-Dole Act on U.S. University Research and Technology Transfer," in Lewis M. Branscomb, Fumio Kodama, and Richard Florida, eds., *Industrializing Knowledge: University-Industry Linkages in Japan and the United States* (1999), pp. 269, 300. There are still critics who claim that academic scientists have shifted their activities heavily from basic to applied research, for example, Linda Marsa, *Prescription for Profits: How the Pharmaceutical Industry Bankrolled the Unholy Marriage Between Science and Business* (1997), pp. 7,

143. But these accounts seem to be based on anecdotal evidence rather than a careful review of overall funding for scientific research.

7. Eric C. Campbell and David Blumenthal, "Relationships in Biotechnology: A Primer on Policy and Practice," *Cloning* 2 (2000), p. 103; see also Karen S. Louis, David Blumenthal, Michael E. Gluck, and Michael A. Stoto, "Entrepreneurs in Academe: An Exploration of Behaviors among Life Scientists," *Administrative Science Quarterly* 34 (1989), pp. 110, 115.

8. David Blumenthal, Eric G. Campbell, Nancyanne Causino, and Lauren S. Louis, "Participation of Life Science Faculty in Research Relationships with Industry," *New England Journal of Medicine* 335 (1996), p. 1734.

9. Ibid.

10. David Blumenthal and Eric G. Campbell, "Academic Industry Relationships in Biotechnology, Overview," in Thomas J. Murray and Maxwell J. Mehlman, eds., *Encyclopedia of Ethical, Legal and Policy Issues in Biotechnology* (2000), pp. 1, 6.

11. Ibid.

12. Karen S. Louis et al., "Entrepreneurs in Academe," p. 127.

13. U.S. Department of Education, *National Center for Educational Statistics, Background Characteristics, Work Activities, and Compensation of Faculty and Instructional Staff in Postsecondary Institutions: Fall 1998* (April, 2001), pp. 46 et seq.

14. Ibid.

15. Lisa-Marie Jones, *The Commercialization of Academic Science: Conflict of Interest for the Faculty Consultant*, Ph.D. diss. UMI Pro Quest Digital Dissertations, AAT9986421 (2000), pp. 73–74.

16. Henry Etzkowitz, "Bridging the Gap: The Evolution of Industry-University Links in the United States," in Lewis M. Branscomb, Fumio Kodama, and Richard Florida, eds., *Industrializing Knowledge*, p. 208.

17. See more generally Michael Gibbons et al., *The New Production of Knowledge* (1994).

18. For some interesting findings along these lines, see Eric G. Campbell et al., "Data Withholding in Academic Genetics," *Journal of the American Medical Association* 287 (2000), pp. 473, 478.

19. Mildred K. Cho et al., "Policies on Faculty Conflicts of Interest at U.S. Universities," *Journal of the American Medical Association* 284 (2000), p. 2203.

20. David Blumenthal, Eric G. Campbell et al., "Withholding Research Results in Academic Life Science," *Journal of the American Medical Association* 277 (1997), p. 1224.

21. Ibid.

22. David Blumenthal and Eric G. Campbell, "Academic Industry Relationships," pp. 1, 6.

23. Ibid. See also, Eric G. Campbell, Joel S. Weissmann, Nancyanne Causino, and David Blumenthal, "Data Withholding in Academic Medicine: Characteristics of Faculty Denied Access to Research Results and Biomaterials," *Research Policy* 29 (2000), p. 303.

24. *Report of the National Institutes of Health (NIH) Working Group on Research Tools* (June 4, 1998), p. 18.

25. Ibid.

26. Association of American Medical Colleges, "Guidelines for Dealing with Conflicts of Commitment and Conflicts of Interest in Research," *Academic Medicine* 65 (1990), p. 491.

27. See, for example, H. T. Stelfox et al., "Conflict of Interest in the Debate over Calcium Channel Antagonists," *New England Journal of Medicine* 338 (1998), p. 101; P.A. Rochon et al., "A Study of Manufacturer-Supported Trials of Nonsteroidal Anti-inflammatory Drugs in the Treatment of Arthritis," *Archives of Internal Medicine* 154 (1994), p. 157; and Deborah A. Barnes and Lisa A. Bero, "Why Review Articles on the Health Effects of Passive Smoking Reach Different Conclusions," *Journal of the American Medical Association* 279 (1998), p. 1566.

28. For example, a recent review of clinical studies of new drugs to fight cancer revealed that 38 percent of the studies fi-

nanced by nonprofit organizations reported unfavorable results, whereas only 5 percent of studies funded by pharmaceutical companies reached unfavorable conclusions. See Mark Friedberg et al., "Evaluation of Conflict of Interest in Economic Analyses of New Drugs Used in Oncology," *Journal of the American Medical Association* 282 (1999), p. 1453. In fairness, it should be pointed out that factors other than financial bias could help to account for these differences. For example, drug companies may be less inclined than other funders to support clinical trials unless they have reason to believe that they will be successful.

29. The arguments are discussed in Roger J. Porter and Thomas E. Malone, eds., *Biomedical Research: Collaboration and Conflict of Interest* (1992). For a vigorous exposition of the arguments against efforts to regulate conflicts of interest, see Kenneth J. Rothman, "Conflict of Interest: The New McCarthyism in Science," *Journal of the American Medical Association* 269 (1993), p. 2782.

30. S. Van McCrary et al., "A National Survey of Policies on Disclosure of Conflicts of Interest in Biomedical Research," *New England Journal of Medicine* 343 (2000), pp. 1621, 1623.

31. Ibid., p. 1625.

32. Bernard Lo, Leslie E. Wolf, and Albiona Berkeley, "Conflict-of-Interest Policies for Investigators in Clinical Trials," *New England Journal of Medicine* 343 (2000), p. 1616.

33. Thomas Bodenheimer, "Uneasy Alliance: Clinical Investigators and the Pharmaceutical Industry," *New England Journal of Medicine* 342 (2000), p. 1539. For a detailed analysis of how studies can be manipulated to arrive at more favorable findings, see Lisa A. Bero and Drummond Rennie, "Influences on the Quality of Published Drug Studies," *International Journal of Technology Assessment in Health Care* 12 (1996), p. 209.

34. One author, Thomas Bodenheimer, seems, on the basis of his informal survey, to imply that such cases are not uncommon; see note 33.

35. Susan Okie, "Journals Decide to Help Fight Firms' Influ-

ence on Research," *International Herald Tribune* (September 11, 2001), p. 3.

36. Ibid.

37. Quoted in Bodenheimer, "Uneasy Alliance," p. 1541

38. Deborah A. Barnes and Lisa A. Bero, "Why Review Articles," p. 1566.

CHAPTER FIVE   EDUCATION

1. The following account of the dealings between U.Next and Columbia is taken from an article by Todd Woody, *"Ivy Online," The Standard: Intelligence for the Internet Economy* (Oct. 22, 1999).

2. Abraham Flexner, *Universities: American, English, German* (1930), pp. 133–47.

3. Walton S. Bittner and Harvey F. Mallory, *University Teaching by Mail: A Survey of Correspondence Instruction Conducted by American Universities* (1933).

4. Ibid., p. 74.

5. See generally Leonard Freedman, *Quality in Continuing Education: Principles, Practices, and Standards* (1987); Philip Frandson, ed., *Power and Conflict in Continuing Education: Survival and Prosperity for All?* (1980); Thomas Singarella and George Boddy, "Profit Generation in Continuing Education Centers in Colleges and Universities," *Journal of Continuing Higher Education* 34 (1986), p. 12.

6. Leonard Freedman, *Quality in Continuing Education*, p. 158; Thomas Singarella and George Boddy, "Profit Generation in Continuing Education," p. 12.

7. See, for example, Jeanne C. Meister, *Corporate Universities: Lessons in Building a World-Class Work Force* (rev. ed., 1998).

8. See generally Albert A. Vicere and Robert M. Fulmer, *Leadership by Design* (1996); Stuart Crainer and Des Dearlove, *Gravy Training: Inside the Business of Business Schools* (1999).

9. See Martin H. Schaffer, "Commercial Support and the

Quandary of Continuing Medical Education," *The Journal of Continuing Education in the Health Professions* 20 (2000), p. 120.

10. See generally Richard N. Katz, ed., *Dancing with the Devil: Information Technology and the New Competition in Higher Education* (1998).

11. Nina Schuyler, "Class Dismissed?" *Stanford* (May 2001), p. 61.

12. harvard.net.news (May 21, 1998), p. 1.

13. Robert Lenzner and Stephen S. Johnson, "Seeing Things as They Really Are," *Forbes* (March 10, 1997), p. 122.

14. Quoted in Marc J. Rosenberg, *e-learning* (2001), p. 20.

15. Quoted in Barbara L. Watkins and Stephen J. Wright, eds., *The Foundations of American Distance Education: A Century of Collegiate Correspondence Study* (1991), p. 25.

16. Ibid., p. 138.

17. See generally Otto Peters, *Learning and Teaching in Distance Education; Analyses and Interpretations from an International Perspective* (1998).

18. See, for example, T. L. Russell, "The 'No Significant Difference Phenomenon,'" http:/cuda.teleeducation.nb.ca/nosignificantdifference/; R. A. Phipps and J. P. Merisotis, *What's the Difference?: A Review of Contemporary Research on the Effectiveness of Distance Learning in Higher Education* (1999). Most careful analysts find substantial methodological flaws in existing research on the effectiveness of e-learning.

19. Quoted by Murray Sperber in *Beer and Circus: How Big-Time College Sports Is Crippling Undergraduate Education* (2000), pp. 77–78.

20. See, for example, John Seely Brown and Paul Duguid, "Universities in the Digital Age," *Change* (July 1996), p. 11.

21. See, for example, Trace A. Urdan and Cornelia C. Weggen, *Corporate E-Learning: Exploring a New Frontier* (2000).

22. Michael Goldstein, "To Be (For-Profit) or Not to Be: What Is the Question?" *Change* 33 (Sept.–Oct. 2000), p. 24. (Appar-

ently, Mr. Goldstein does not consider the quality and nature of instruction via Internet to be part of "the question.")

23. Gary Rhoades, "Whose Property Is It? Negotiating with the University," *Academe* 87 (Sept.–Oct., 2001), pp. 38, 43. See also National Education Association, *Leadership Manual: Technology, Bargaining, Policy, and Costs* (2001), p. 28: "Most teachers in this new system will be part-time and have no decision-making power."

24. "Digital Diploma Mills: The Automation of Higher Education," http//www.communication.ucsd.edu/dl/ddmd.html.

25. Ibid.

26. See, for example, Otto Peters, *Learning and Teaching in Distance Education*.

CHAPTER SIX THE BENEFITS AND COSTS OF COMMERCIALIZATION

1. See, for example, Gary W. Matkin, *Technology Transfer and the University* (1990); and Linda Marsa, *Prescription for Profits: How the Pharmaceutical Industry Bankrolled the Unholy Marriage between Science and Business* (1997).

2. Sarah E. Turner shows how schools of education provide mediocre courses at low cost, because most school authorities care about obtaining the proper educational credentials but not about the quality of the courses. See her "The Evolving Production Functions of Schools of Education," in William G. Tierney, ed., *Faculty Work in Schools of Education: Rethinking Roles and Rewards for the Twenty-First Century* (2001), p. 103.

3. Herman Hesse, *Magister Ludi, The Glass Bead Game*, English translation by Richard and Clara Winston, (1969).

4. Ami Zusman, "Issues Facing Higher Education in the Twenty-First Century," in Phillip G. Altbach, Robert O. Berdahl, and Patricia J. Gumport, eds., *American Higher Education in the Twenty-First Century* (1999), pp. 109, 142; to the same effect, see

Clark Kerr, *Higher Education Cannot Escape History: Issues for the Twenty-First Century* (1995).

5. Two directors of labor relations institutes claim that this has already occurred. See Kate Bronfenbrenner and Ted Jurawich, "Universities Should Cease Hostilities with Unions," *The Chronicle of Higher Education* (Jan. 19, 2001), p. B24.

CHAPTER SEVEN REFORMING ATHLETICS

1. Walter Byers, *Unsportsmanlike Conduct: Exploiting College Athletes* (1995).

2. Andrew Zimbalist, *Unpaid Professionals: Commercialism and Conflict in Big-Time College Sports* (1999), p. 199.

3. Knight Foundation Commission on Intercollegiate Athletics, *Reconnecting College Sports and Higher Education* (2001), p. 38.

4. James L. Shulman and William G. Bowen, *The Game of Life: College Sports and Educational Values* (2001), p. 313.

5. Ibid., p. 319.

CHAPTER EIGHT PROTECTING THE INTEGRITY OF RESEARCH

1. Quoted in Charles Weiner, "Universities, Professors, and Patents: A Continuing Controversy," *Technology Review* (Feb.–Mar. 1986), p. 35. See also Gary W. Matkin, *Technology Transfer and the University* (1990), pp. 56.

2. Norbert Wiener, *Invention: The Care and Feeding of Ideas* (1993), p. 151.

3. I do not mean to imply any approval or disapproval of trends in the scope of patentability as defined by the Supreme Court in decisions such as *Diamond v. Chakrabarty*, 447 U.S. 303 (1980).

4. The proportion of research contracts containing questionable provisions may be as great as one-third or more. See Thomas

Bodenheimer, "Uneasy Alliance: Clinical Investigators and the Pharmaceutical Industry," *New England Journal of Medicine* 342 (2000), pp. 1539, 1541.

5. Bernard Lo, Leslie E. Wolf, and Albiona Berkeley, "Conflicts-of-Interest Policies for Investigators in Clinical Trials," *New England Journal of Medicine* 343 (2000), p. 1616.

6. Sheldon Krimsky and L. S. Rothenberg, "Conflict of Interest Policies in Science and Medical Journals: Editorial Practices and Author Disclosures," *Science and Engineering Ethics* 7 (2001), p. 205.

7. It is true that universities have prohibited their researchers from entering into other relationships with corporations, such as agreeing to overly broad secrecy requirements. But secrecy, unlike financial conflicts of interest, does not simply create a risk of bias that can be countered by disclosure and debate. It does damage to collegiality, trust, and other aspects of the academic enterprise that no amount of disclosure or scientific rebuttal can undo.

8. For a fuller discussion of this problem, see Ezekiel J. Emanuel and Daniel Steiner, "Institutional Conflicts of Interest," *New England Journal of Medicine* 332 (1995), p. 262.

9. M. M. Chren and C. S. Landefeld, "Physicians' Behavior and Their Interactions with Drug Companies," *Journal of the American Medical Association* 271 (1994), p. 684; R. A. Davidson, "Source of Funding and Outcome of Clinical Trials," *Journal of General Internal Medicine* 1 (1986), p. 155; H. T. Stelfox et al., "Conflict of Interest in the Debate over Calcium-Channel Antagonists," *New England Journal of Medicine* 338 (1998), p. 101.

10. Robert Sanders, "CNR, Novartis Seal $25 Million Biotech Research Agreement," *Berkeleyan* (Dec. 2, 1998), p. 1.

11. Goldie Blumenstyk, "A Vilified Corporate Partnership Produces Little Change (Except Better Facilities)," *Chronicle of Higher Education* (June 22, 2001), p. A24.

12. See, for example, Derek Bok, *Beyond the Ivory Tower: Social Responsibilities of the Modern University* (1982), p. 136.

13. Josh Lerner, "Venture Capital and the Commercialization of Academic Technology: Symbiosis and Paradox," in Lewis Branscomb, Fumio Kodama, and Richard Florida, eds., *Industrializing Knowledge: University-Industry Linkages in Japan and the United States* (1999), p. 405.

14. Rikard Stankiewicz, *Academics and Entrepreneurs: Developing University-Industry Relations* (1986), p. 113.

CHAPTER NINE PRESERVING EDUCATIONAL VALUES

1. Sarah E. Turner, "The Evolving Production Functions of Schools of Education," in William G. Tierney, ed., *Faculty Work in Schools of Education: Rethinking Roles and Rewards for the Twenty-First Century* (2001), p. 103.

2. For example, see Stuart Crainer and Des Dearlove, *Gravy Training: Inside the Business of Business Schools* (1999). Among the business school professors quoted are Philip Kotler of Northwestern University: "Business schools have managed to create an aura of respectability to cover up what is otherwise a bloody brawl. They have given intellectual respectability to what is otherwise folk wisdom" (p. 1). Peter Drucker adds: "The business schools of the U.S. set up less than a century ago have been preparing well-trained clerks" (p. 10).

3. Michael J. Roberts and Howard H. Stevenson, *HBS Background Brief: The Evolving Market for Business Education* (Feb. 2, 2001), p. 3.

4. See generally Otto Peters, *Learning and Teaching in Distance Education: Analyses and Interpretations from an International Perspective* (1998). Mr. Peters points out that "what is no longer needed are large-scale courses for as many students as possible, but a variety of courses with low numbers where the course content is constantly being updated" (p. 114). Much of Peters's book is an elaboration on this theme, a theme that is as applicable to courses on campus as it is to online courses and other forms of distance learning.

5. The term "hidden curriculum" is taken from Benson R. Snyder's book, *The Hidden Curriculum* (1970).

6. Alex Molnar, *Sponsored Schools and Commercialized Classrooms: Schoolhouse Commercializing Trends in the 1990s* (August 1998), available on-line at *http//www.uwm.edu/Dept/CACE*.

7. For a critical account of the role of pharmaceutical companies in continuing medical education, see Arnold S. Relman, "Separating Continuing Medical Education from Pharmaceutical Marketing," *Journal of the American Medical Association* 285 (2001), p. 2009.

8. Ashley Wazana, "Physicians and the Pharmaceutical Industry: Is a Gift Ever Just a Gift?" *Journal of the American Medical Association* 283 (2000), p. 373.

9. See National Survey of Student Engagement, *2001 NSSE Viewpoint* (2001), p. 8.

10. National Center for Public Policy and Higher Education, *Measuring Up 2000: The State-By-State Report Card for Higher Education* (2000). For an account of this and other efforts to measure quality in higher education, see Douglas C. Bennett, "Assessing Quality in Higher Education," *Liberal Education* (Spring 2001), p. 40.

11. See, for example, John A. Centra, *Determining Faculty Effectiveness* (1980), pp. 26–28; Peter Cohen, "Student Ratings of Instruction and Student Achievement: A Meta-Analysis of Multisection Validity Studies," *Review of Educational Research* 51 (1981), p. 281; Frank Costina, William Greenough, and Robert Menges, "Student Ratings of College Teaching: Reliability, Validity, and Usefulness," *Review of Educational Research* 41 (1971), p. 511.

CHAPER TEN LIVING UP TO THE RULES

1. Robert Rosenzweig, *The Political University: Policy, Politics, and Presidential Leadership in the American Research University* (1998), p. 127.

2. See, for example, James J. Duderstadt, *Intercollegiate Athletics and the American University: A University President's Perspective* (2000), pp. 13, 271. "Many trustees are strongly influenced by athletics boosters . . . they too tend to resist proposals for major reform. . . . Many of these trustees become overly close to athletics programs, seeking direct access to coaches, marching with the team to away games, and developing inappropriate relationships with players."

3. James J. Duderstadt, *A University for the 21st Century* (2000), p. 245. According to Duderstadt, a former president of the University of Michigan, "too many trustees of public university boards lack a basic understanding of higher education or a significant commitment to it, understanding neither the concept of service on a board nor their responsibilities to the entire institution."

4. Simon Marginson and Mark Considine, *Power, Governance and Reinvention in Australia* (2000), p. 11.

5. Jan Currie, "Globalization Practices and the Professoriate in Anglo-Pacific Universities," *Comparative Education Review* 42 (1998): 15.

6. Quoted in Todd Woody, "Ivy Online," *The Industry Standard* (1 Nov. 1999), p. 1.

7. Marginson and Considine, *Power, Governance and Reinvention*, p. 237.

8. See, generally, Alex Molnar, *Giving Kids the Business: The Commercialization of America's Schools* (1996).

CHAPTER ELEVEN SEIZING THE MOMENT

1. See James L. Shulman and William G. Bowen, *The Game of Life: College Sports and Educational Values* (2001), p. 311.

2. Karen S. Louis, David Blumenthal et al., "Entrepreneurs in Academe: An Exploration of Behaviors Among Life Scientists," *Administrative Science Quarterly* 24 (1989): 110.

INDEX

A. D. Little, 91

academic community, and effects of commercialization, 113–15

academic freedom, 64–76, 110–13, 148. *See also* academic values; faculty

academic programs, and intercollegiate athletics, 41–46

academic values: and commercial advertising, 177–78; erosion of, 106–14, 172–78, 203; and intercollegiate athletics, 55–56, 129–30; preserving, 206–7

accountability, 30–31; in distance education, 94–95

Adidas, 37

administrators, 4, 19–20, 24–25, 185–87

admissions, 33, 106–7, 134; and student athletes, 39, 41–42

advertising. *See* commercial advertising

agreements, among universities, 193–94, 194n

Akers, Fred, 44

allocation of funds, within university, 163–64, 167–69

alumni offices, 13

antitrust laws, 194n

Apotex, 73–74

Aronowitz, Stanley, 16, 20

assessment, and improvement of teaching, 182

assistance, in improvement of teaching, 183

Association of American Universities, 186

Association of Governing Boards, 129

athletics, intercollegiate, 35–38, 52, 54–56, 98, 102–3, 194; academic costs of, 41–46, 55–56, 120; costs of, 38–39, 100; Division I, 129–35; Divisions II and III, 135–38; high-profile sports, 35–38, 129–33; justifications for, 46–51; "minor" sports, 42n, 133–35; profitability of, 38–39, 54–55; reform of, 53, 123–38; regulation of, 39–41; university presidents and, 51–53. *See also* student athletes

basketball, intercollegiate, 37–38. *See also* athletics, intercollegiate

Bayh-Dole Act (1980), 11–12, 140–41

bias, 75–76, 111–13, 118–21, 145n, 147–48, 175–76. *See also* conflicts of interest

biotechnology industry, 11–12, 151–52. *See also* corporate funding

Boston College, 107

Bowen, William, 39, 41, 49, 136

bowl games, 37

Boyer, Ernest, 49

Boyer, Herbert, 140

buffer organizations, for university investment in faculty enterprises, 153–55